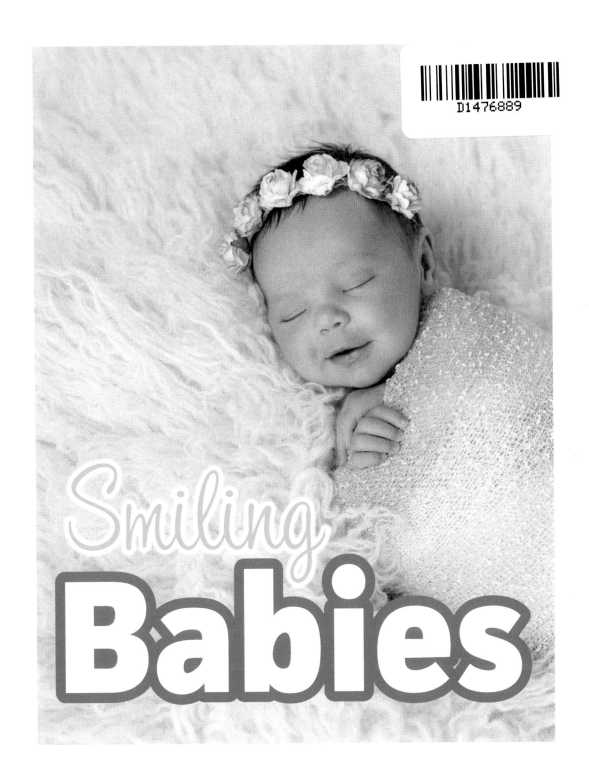

Smiling Babies

Copyright © 2020 by Lasting Happiness
ISBN: 978-1-9995487-4-2

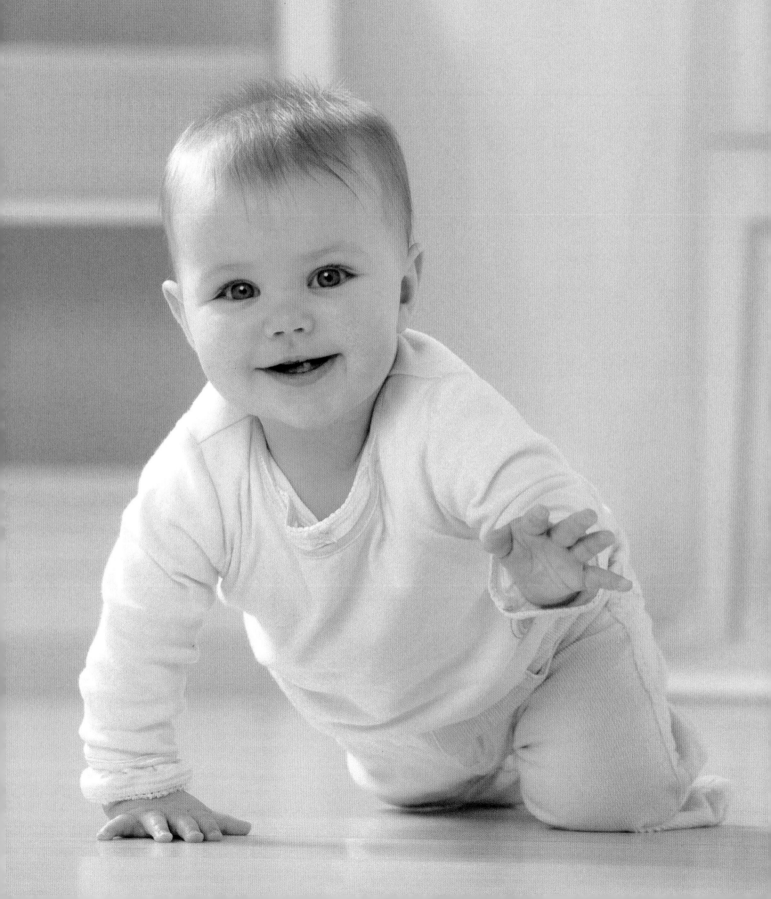

I'm coming, Grandma!

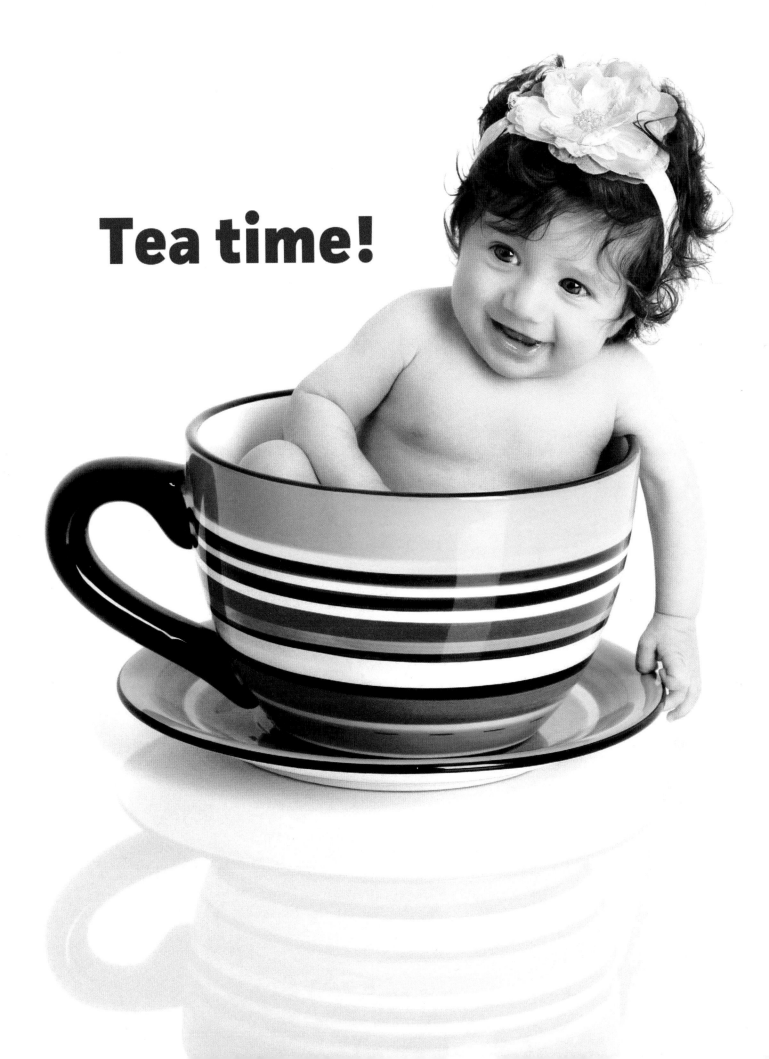

Tea time!

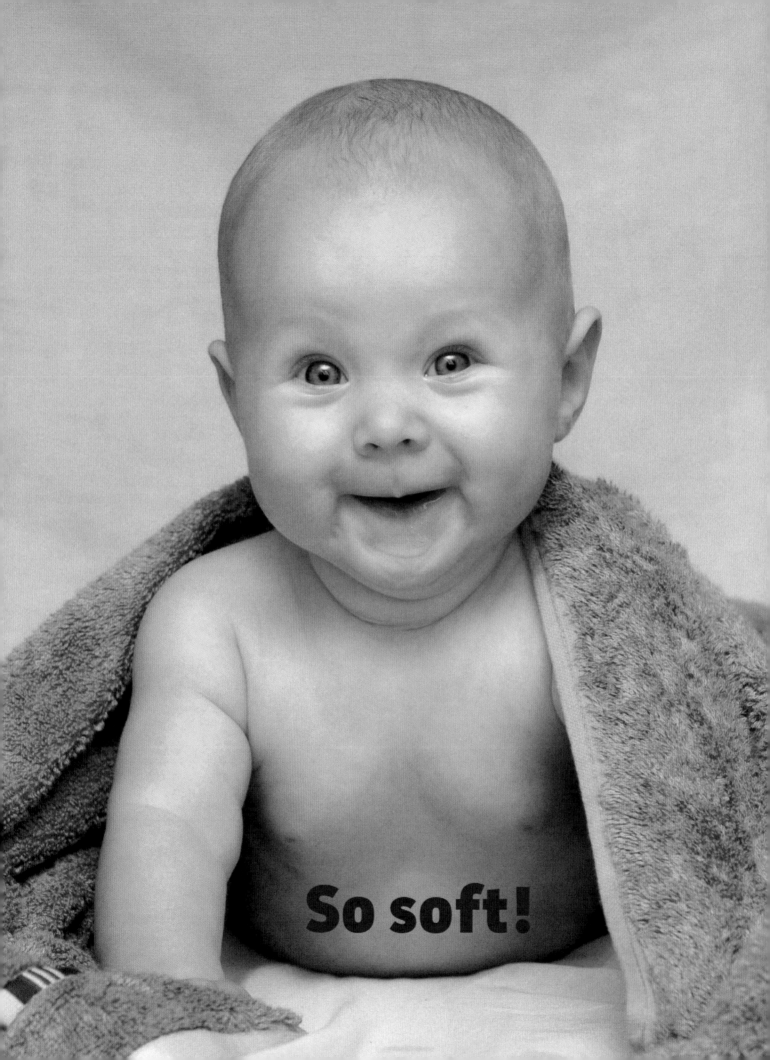

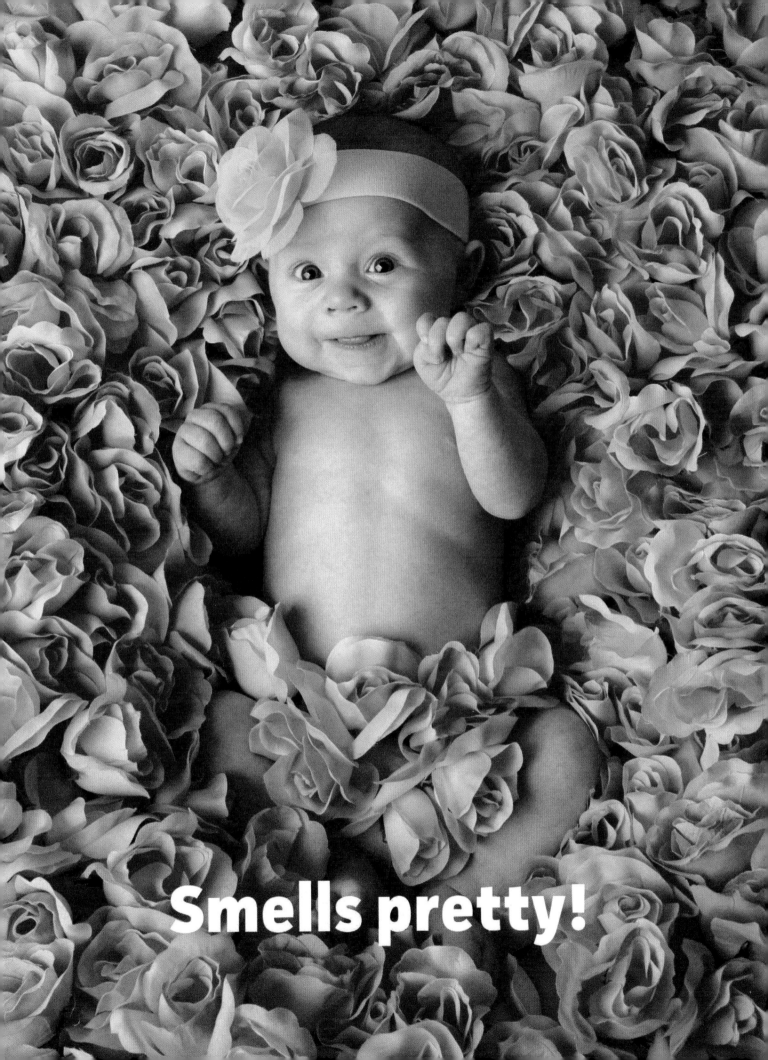

Smells pretty!

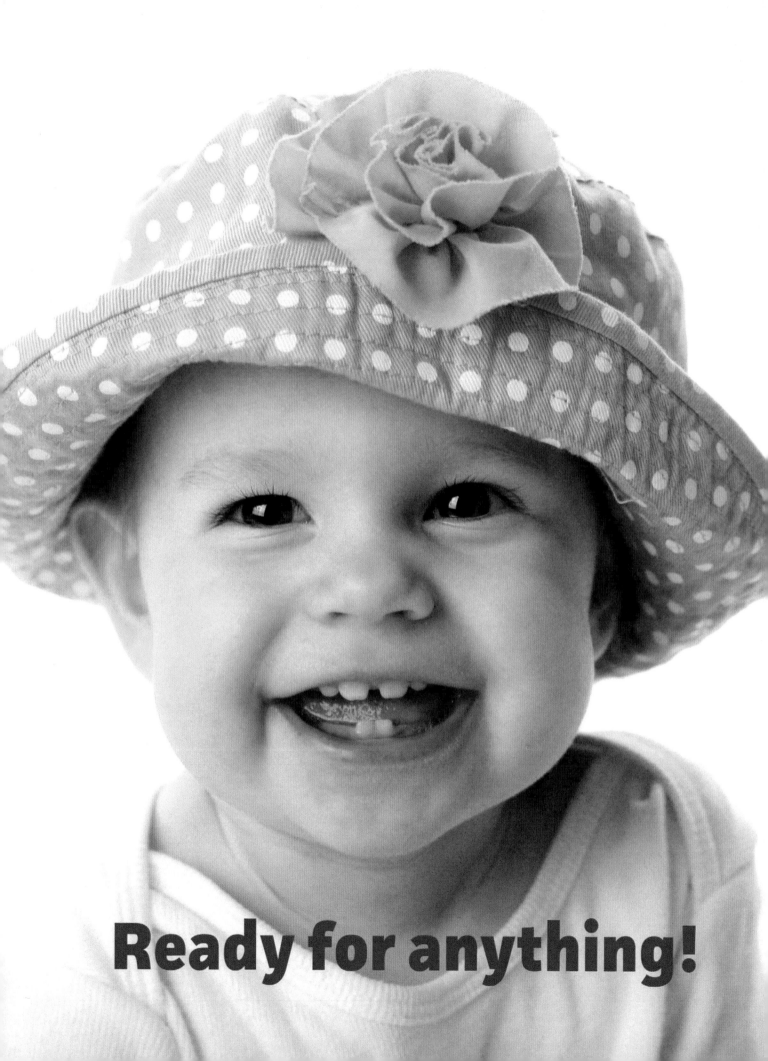

Ready for anything!

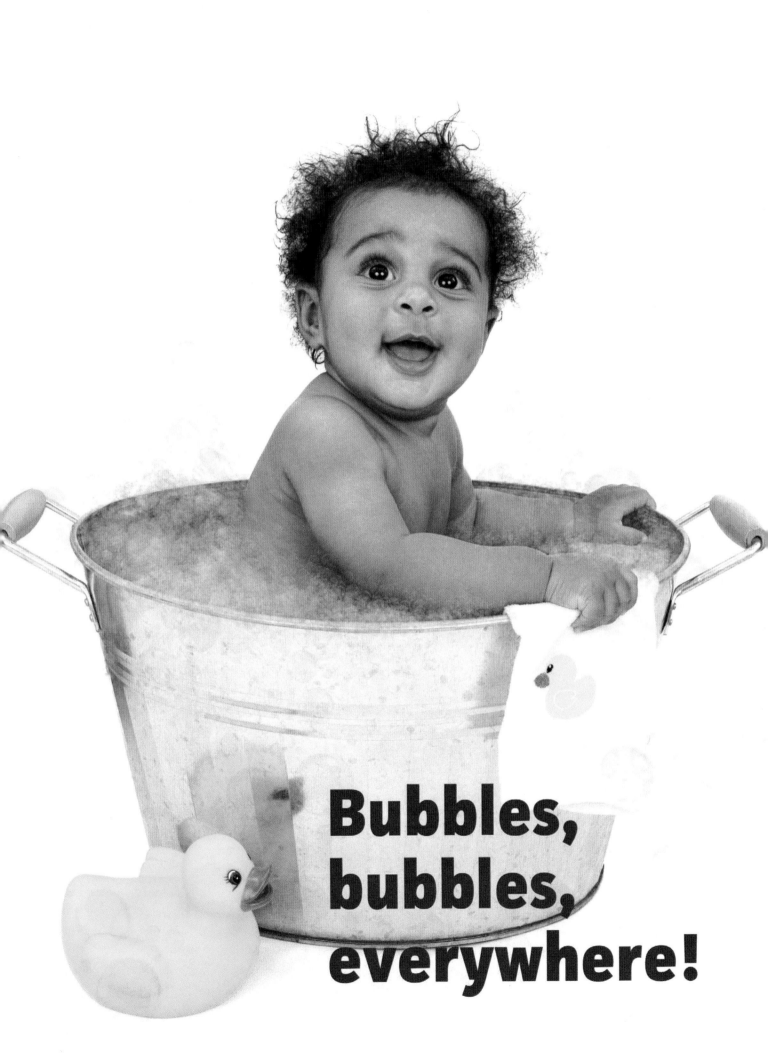

Let's get cooking!

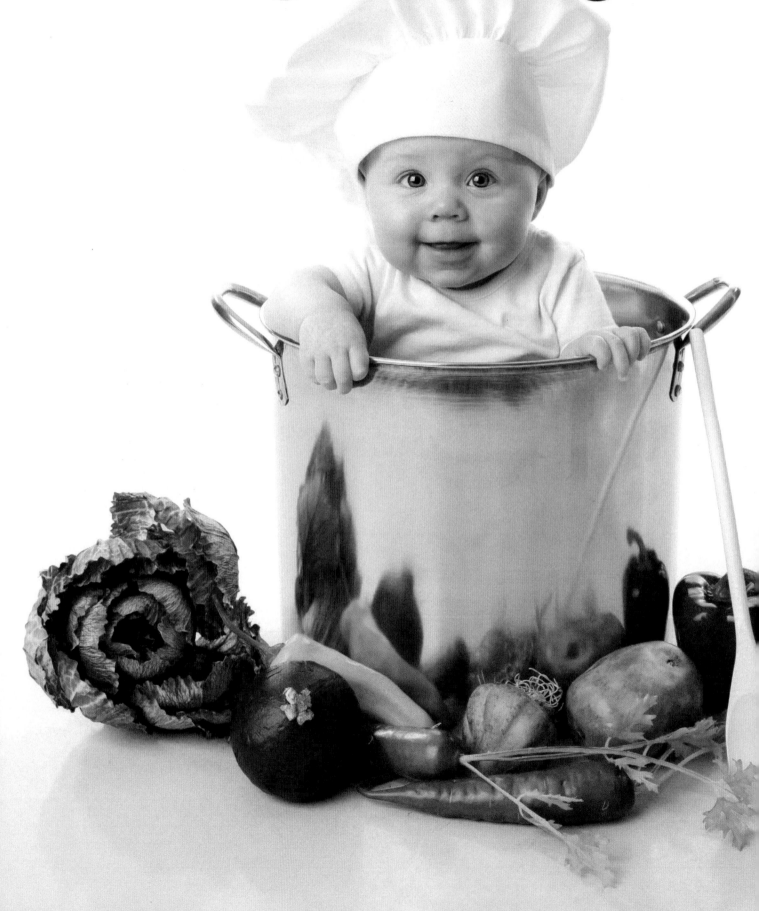

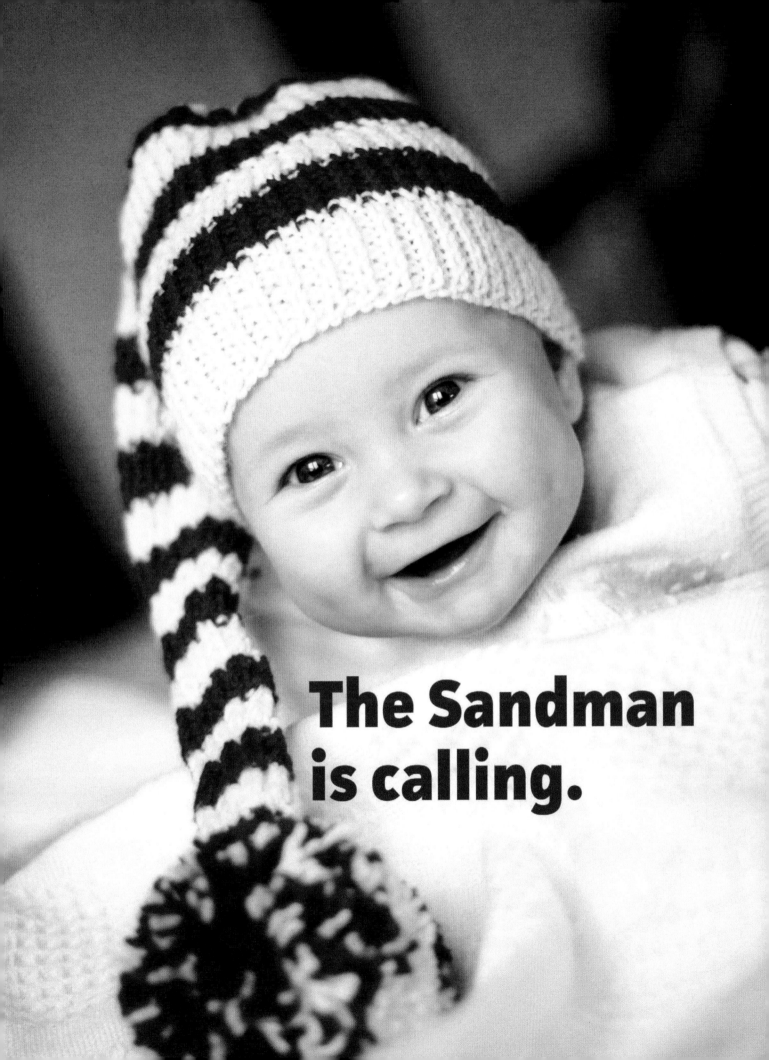

The Sandman is calling.

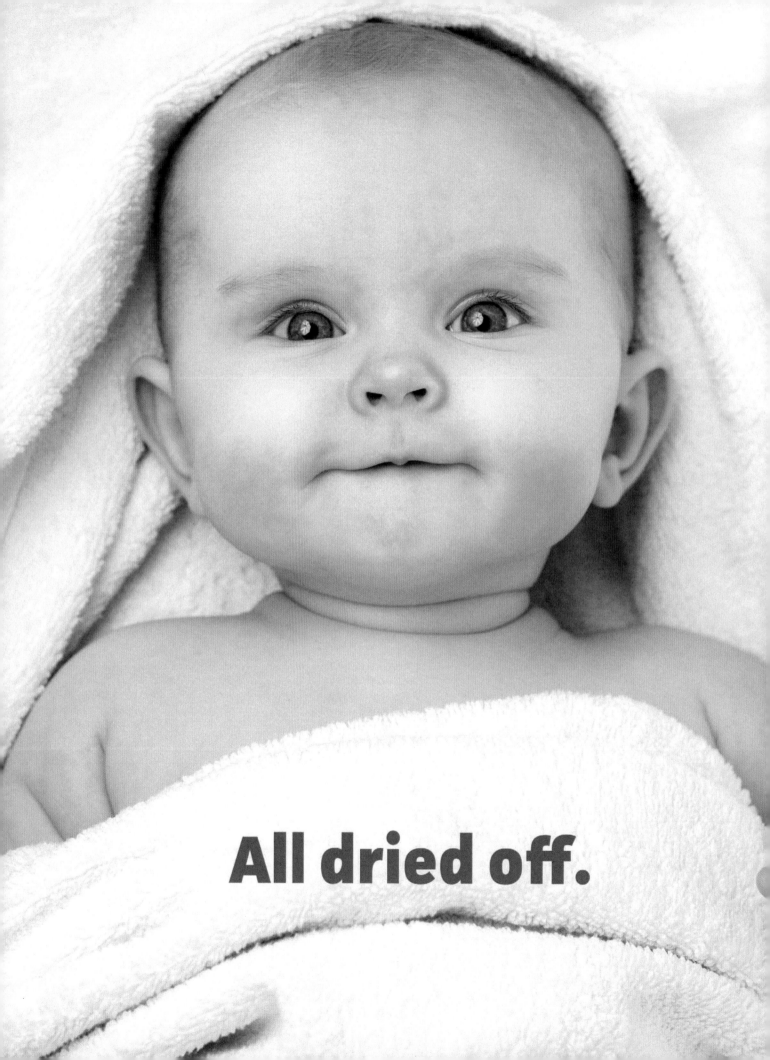

All dried off.

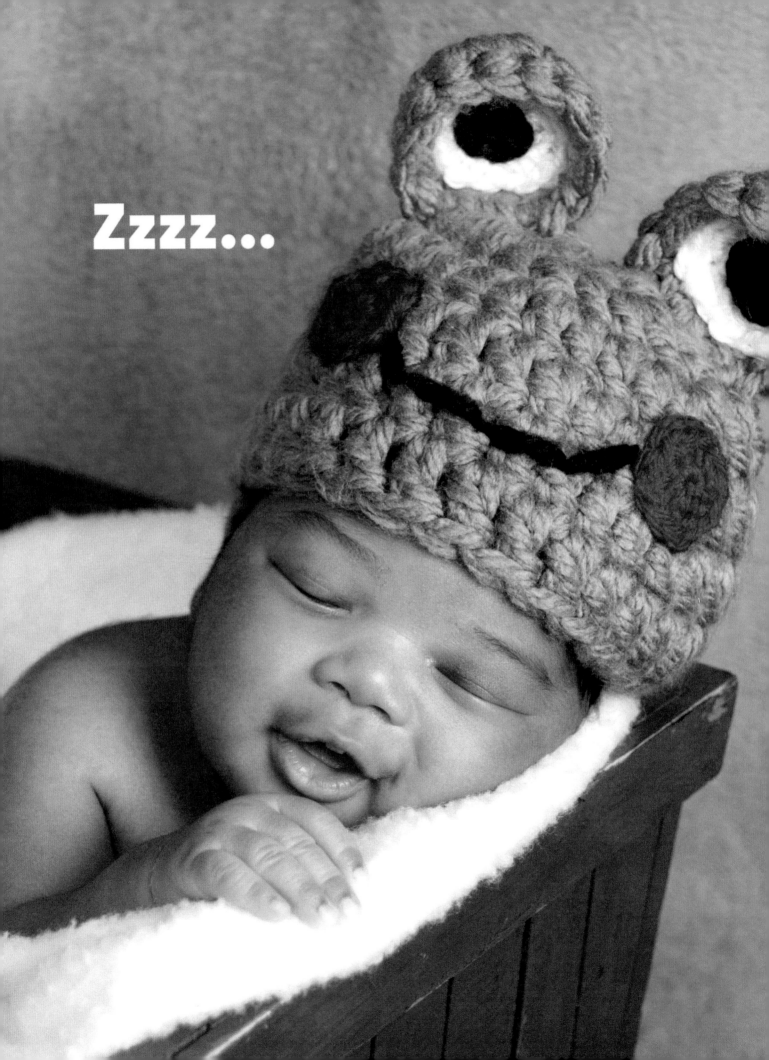
Zzzz...

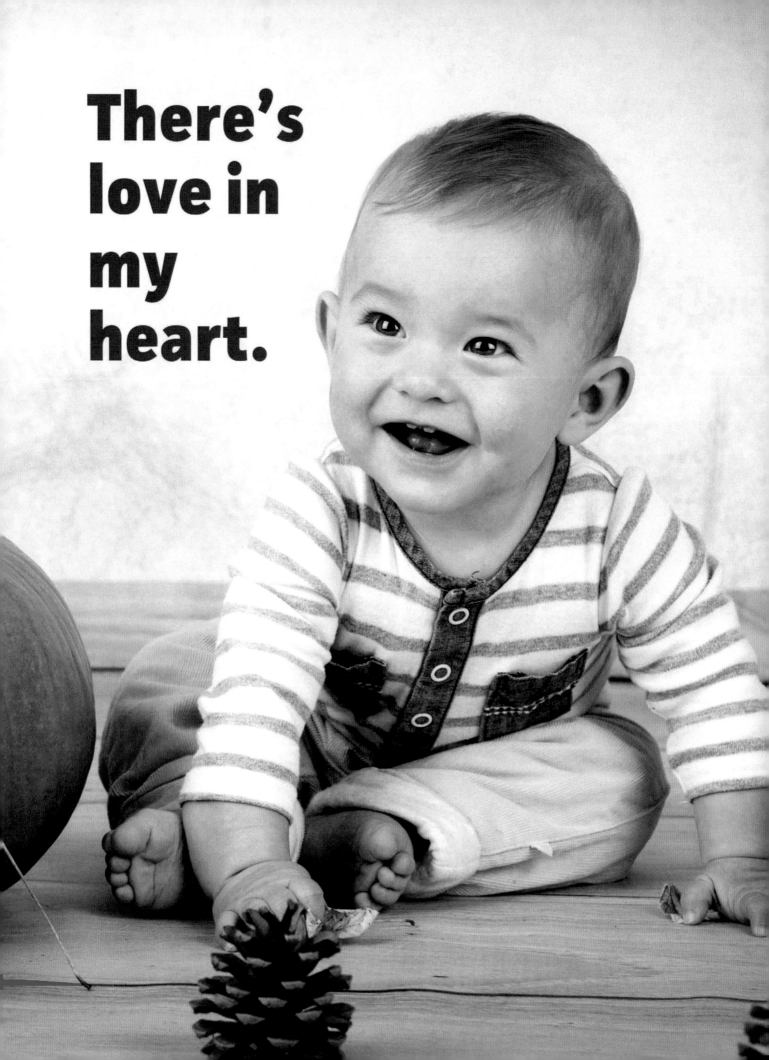

There's love in my heart.

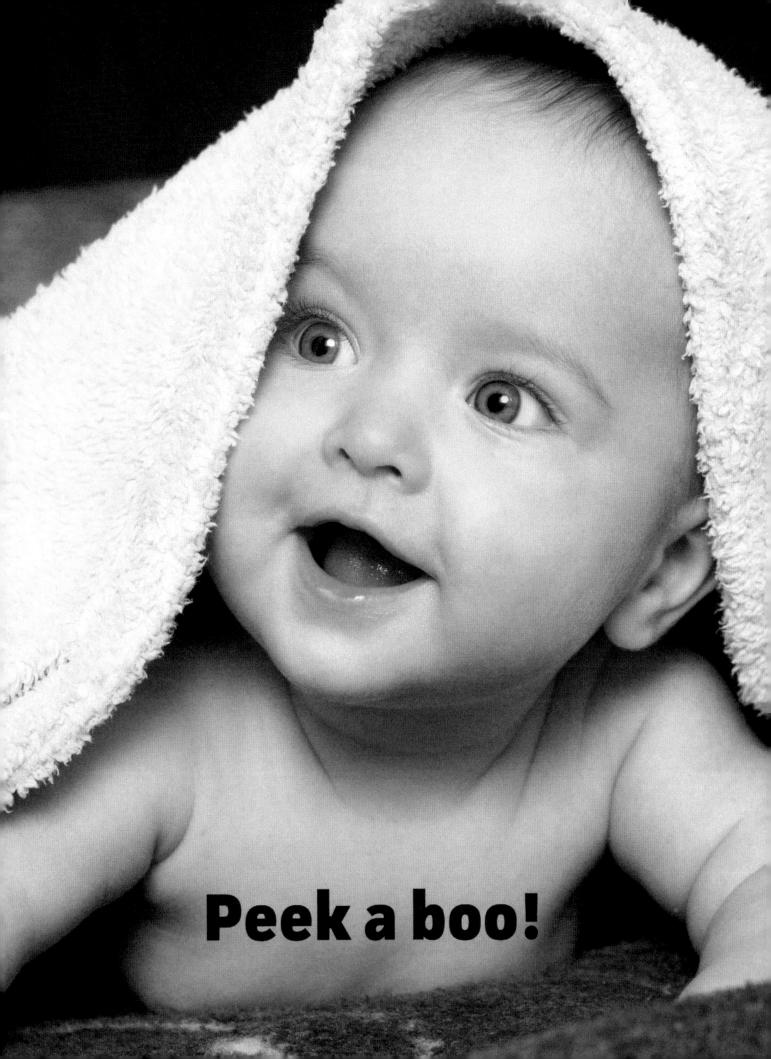

Peek a boo!

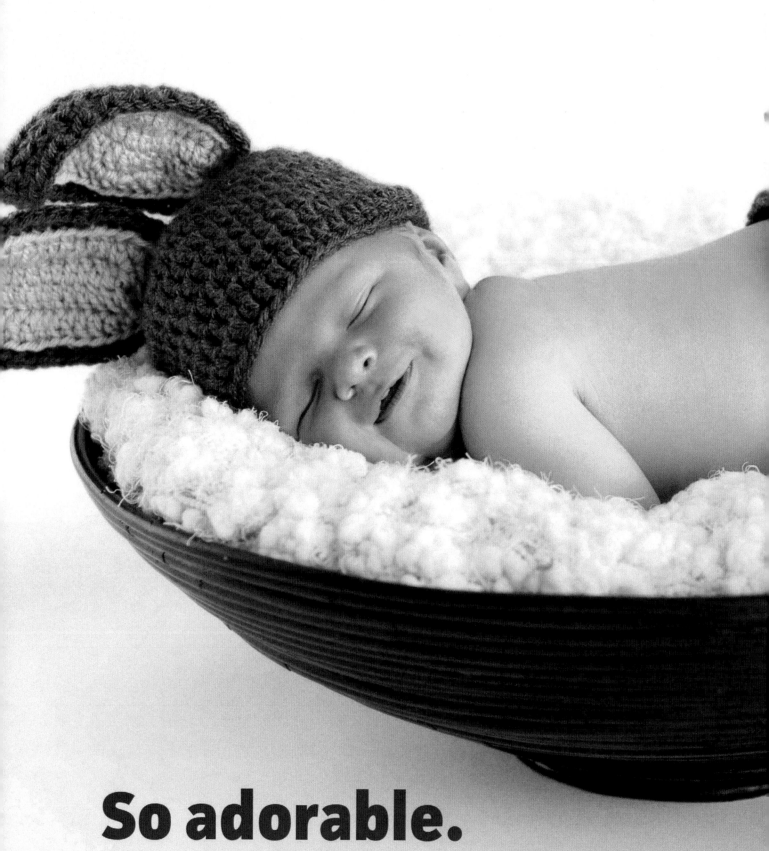

So adorable.

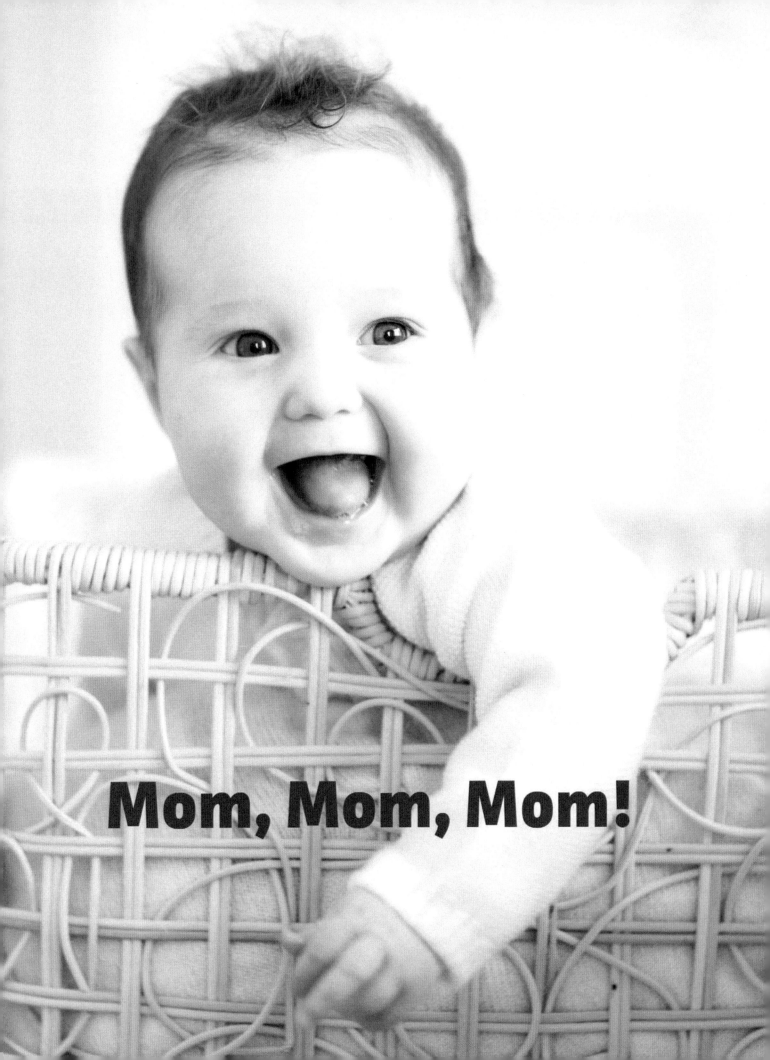

Mom, Mom, Mom!

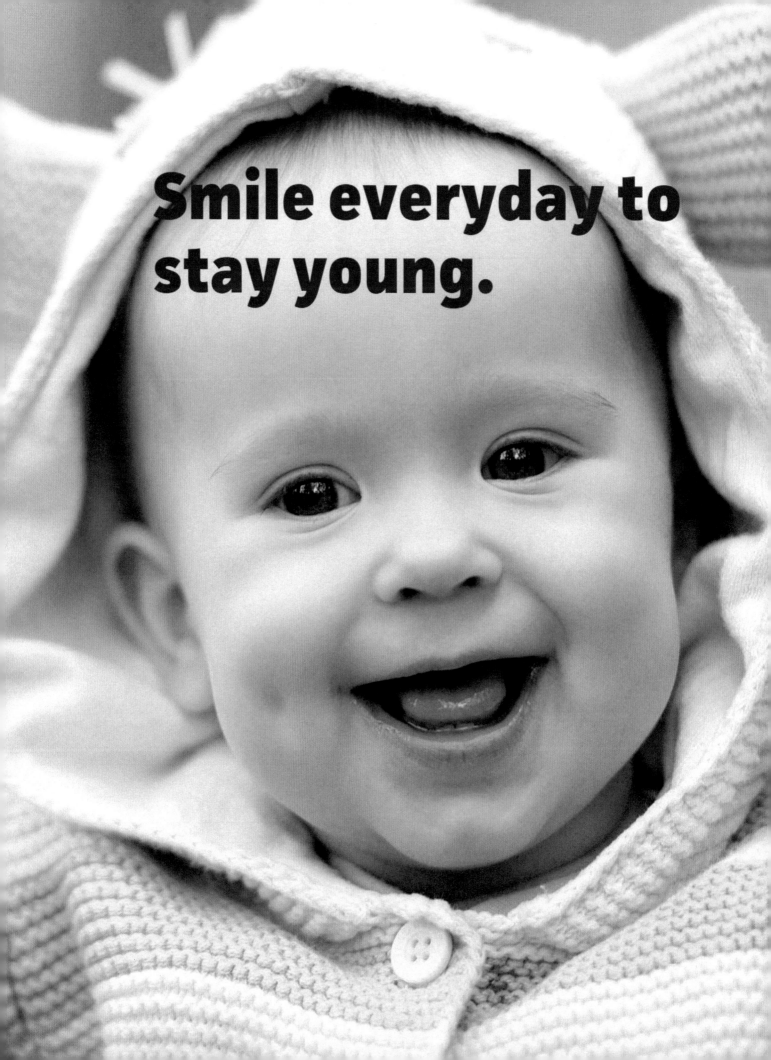

Smile everyday to stay young.

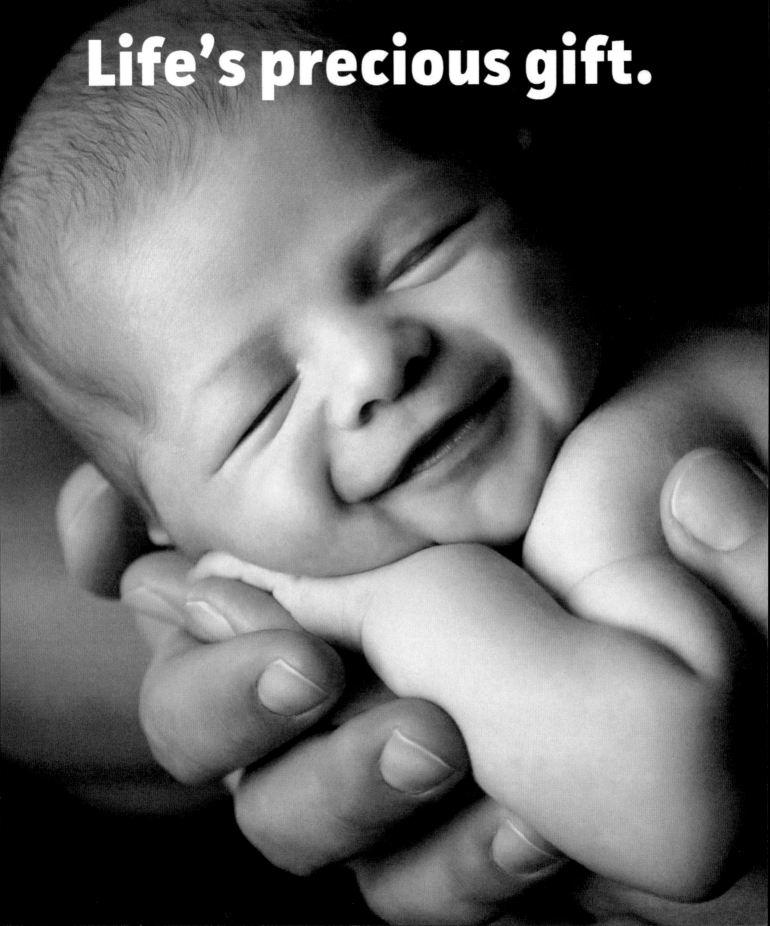

Life's precious gift.

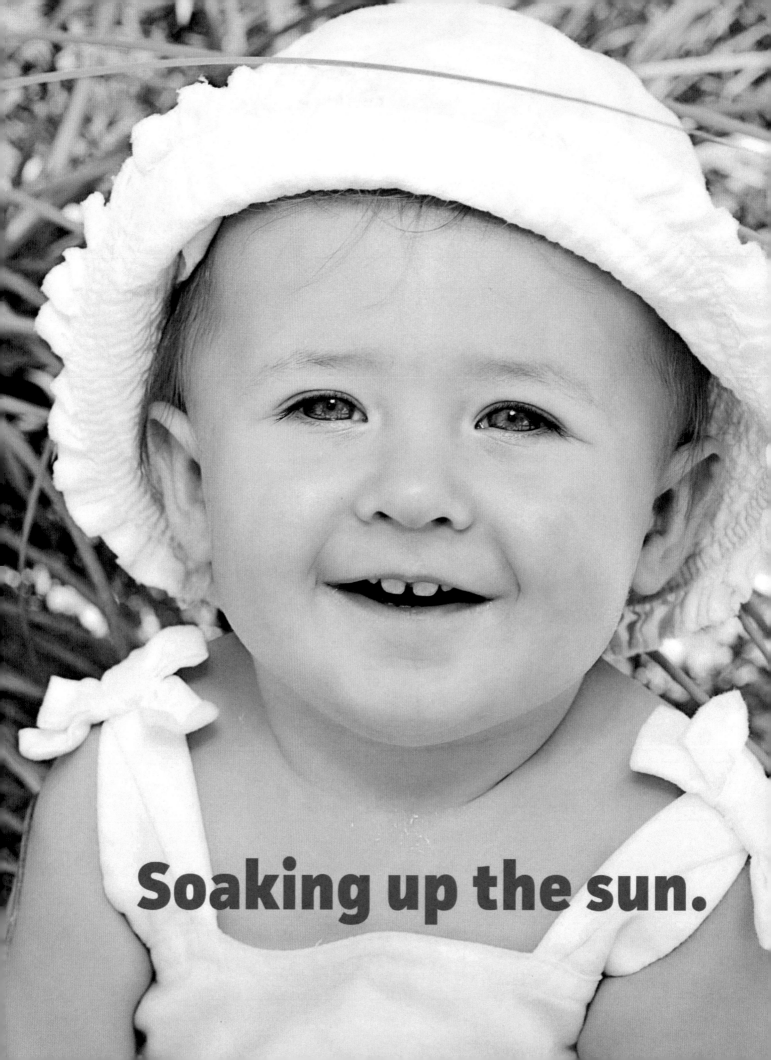

Soaking up the sun.

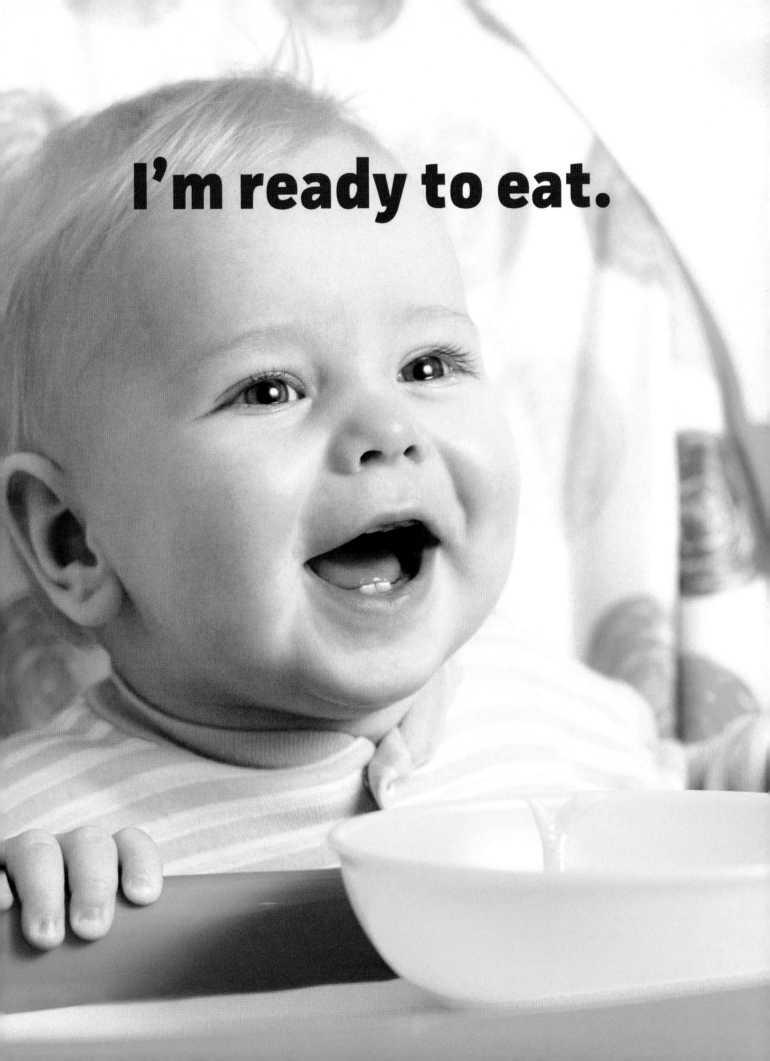

I'm ready to eat.

Born to cook!

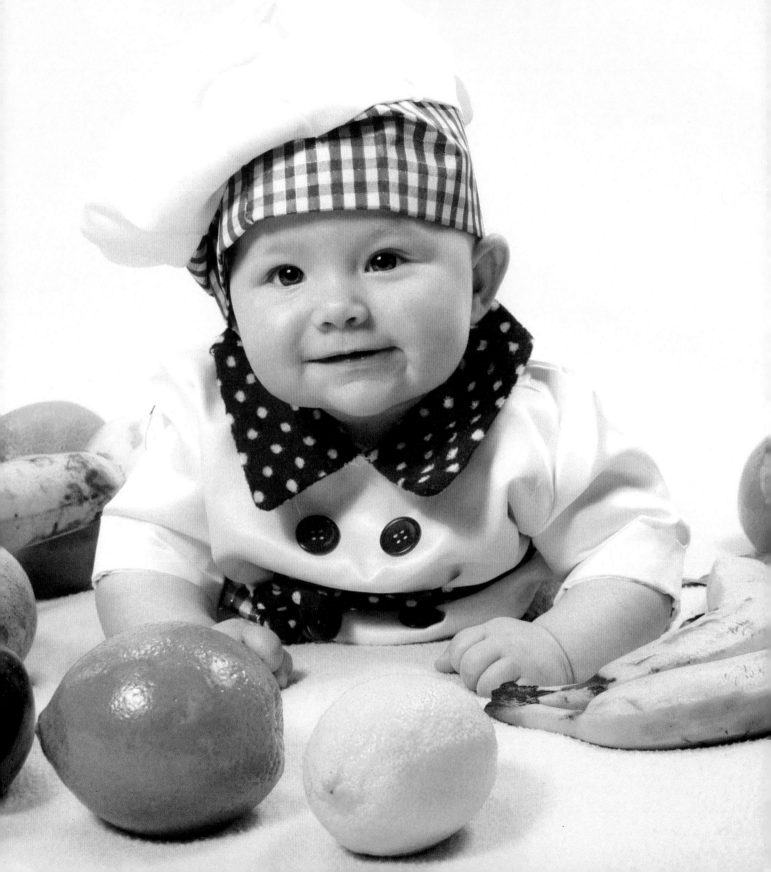

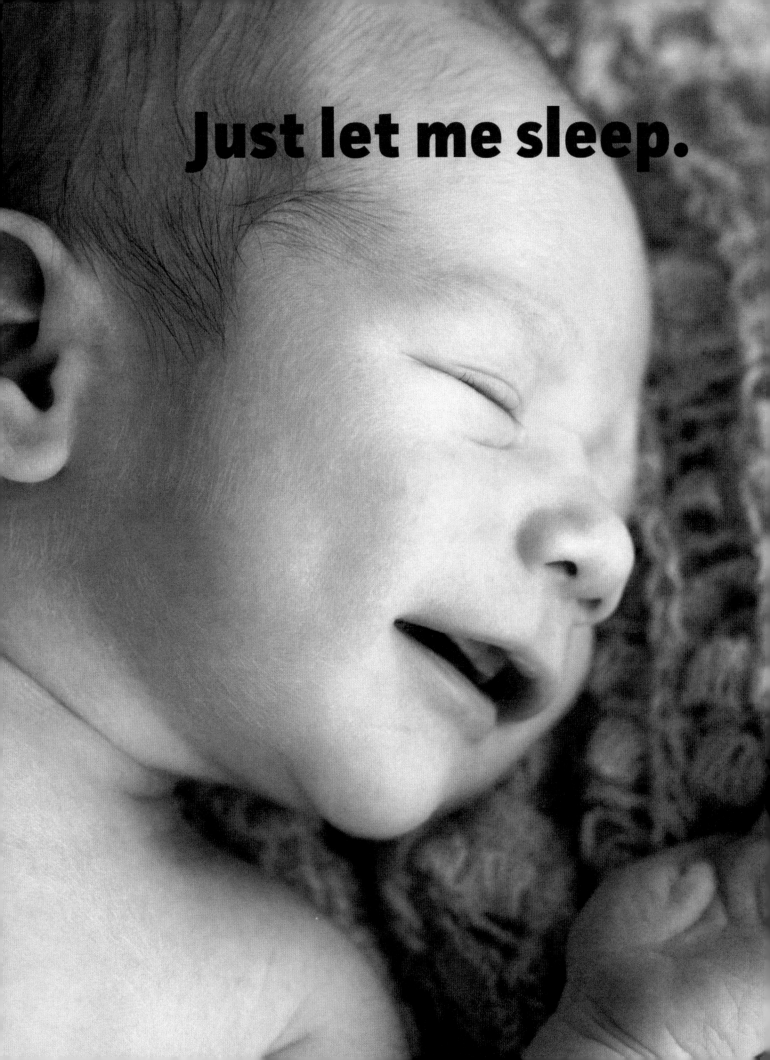

Just let me sleep.

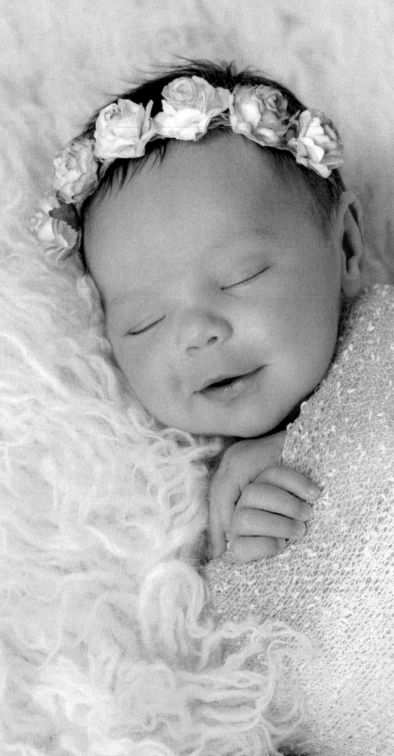

Sweet dreams little one.

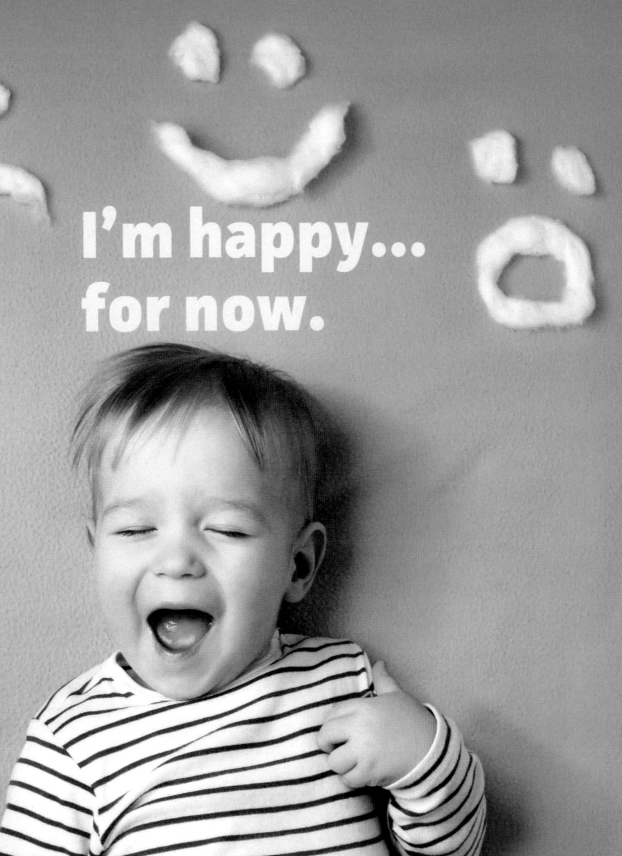

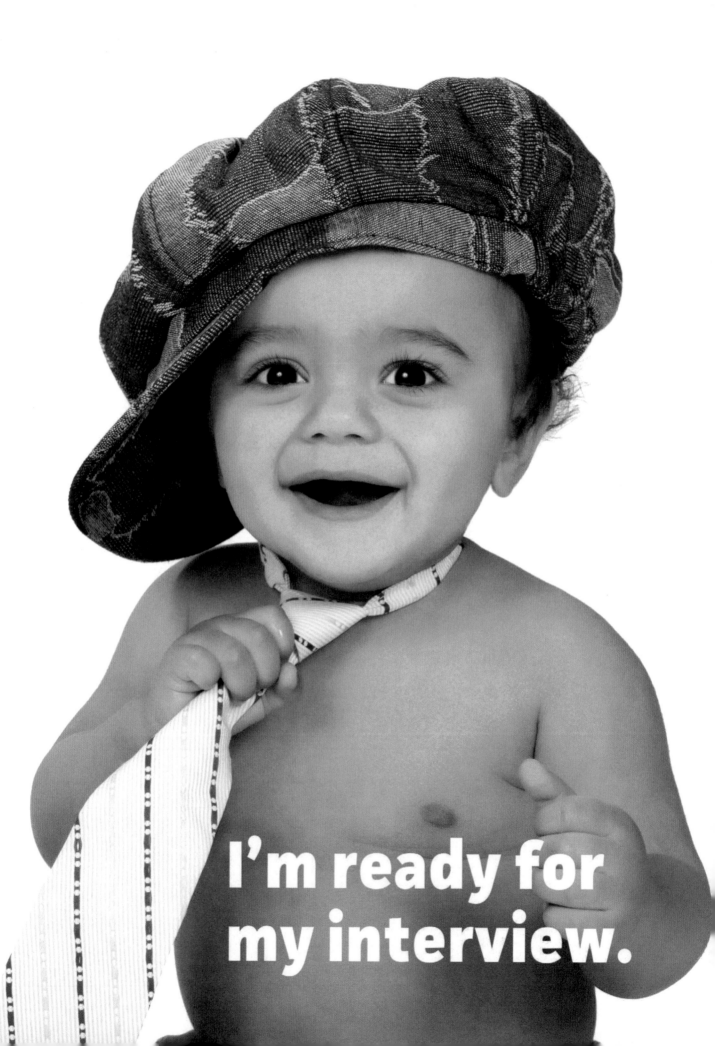

I'm ready for my interview.

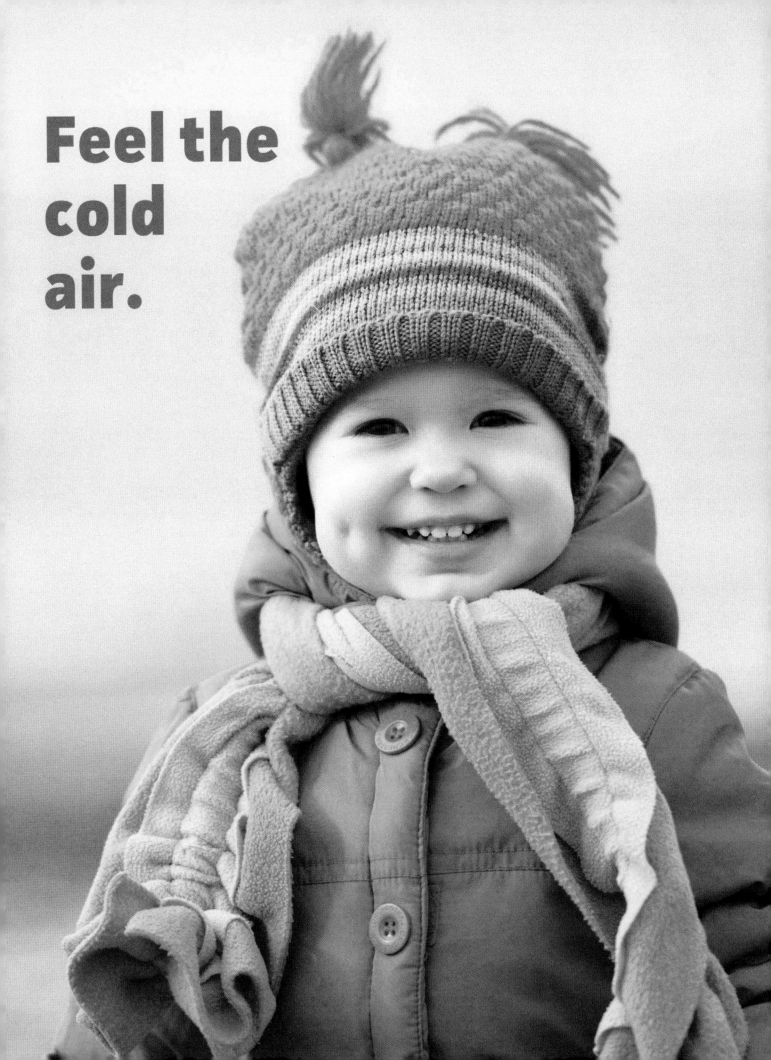

Feel the
cold
air.

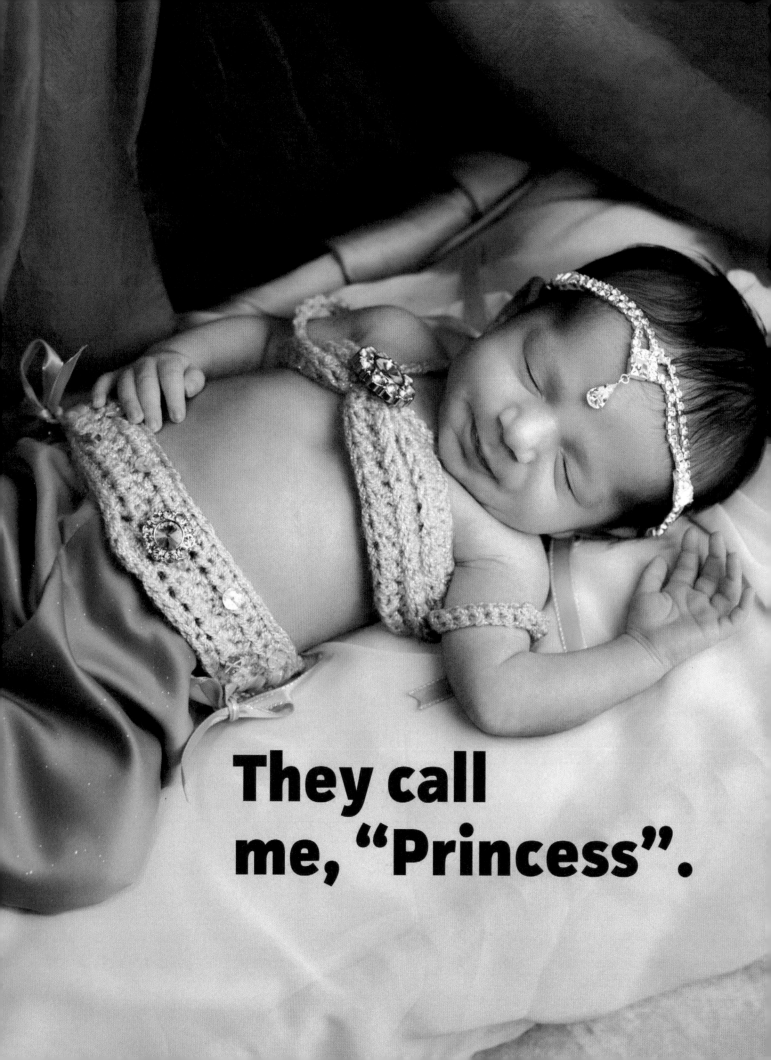

They call me, "Princess".

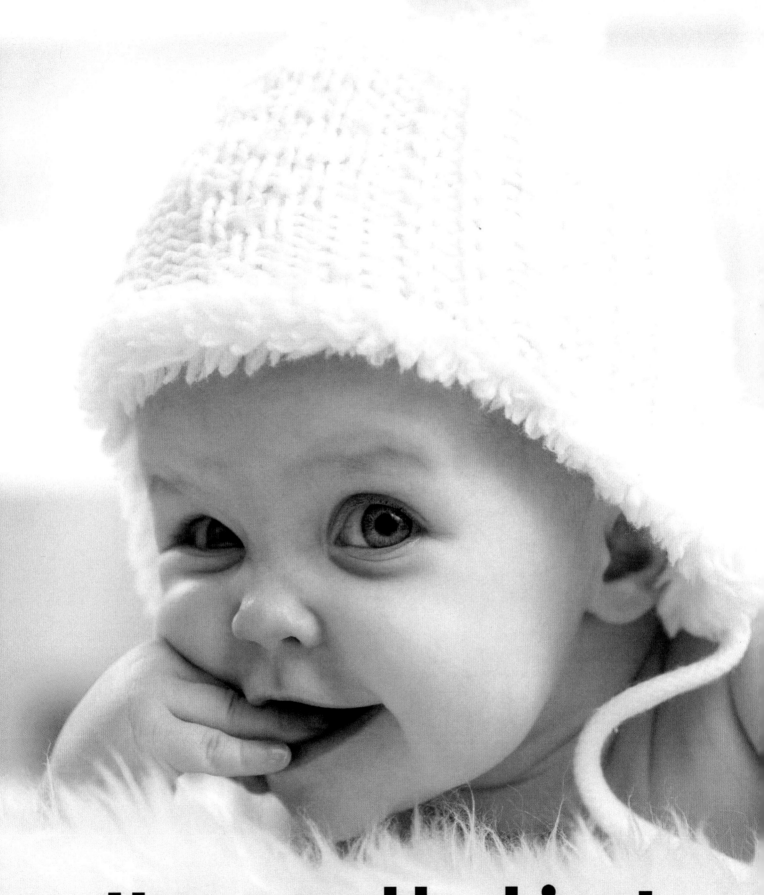

Hey, good looking!

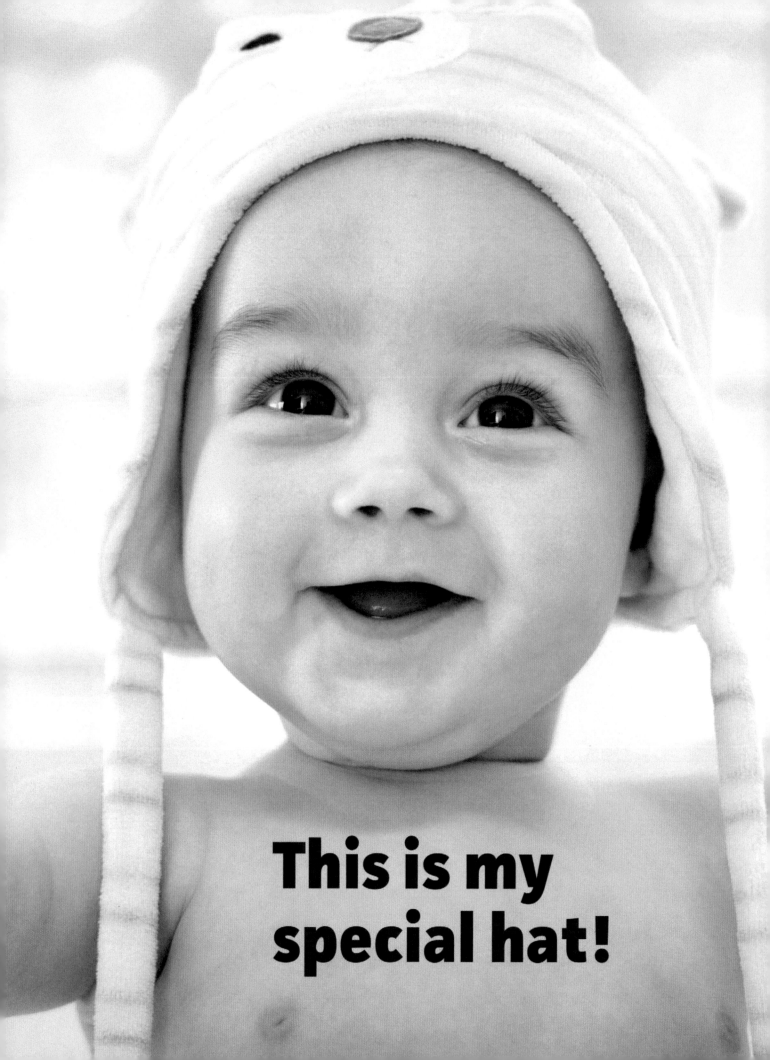

This is my
special hat!

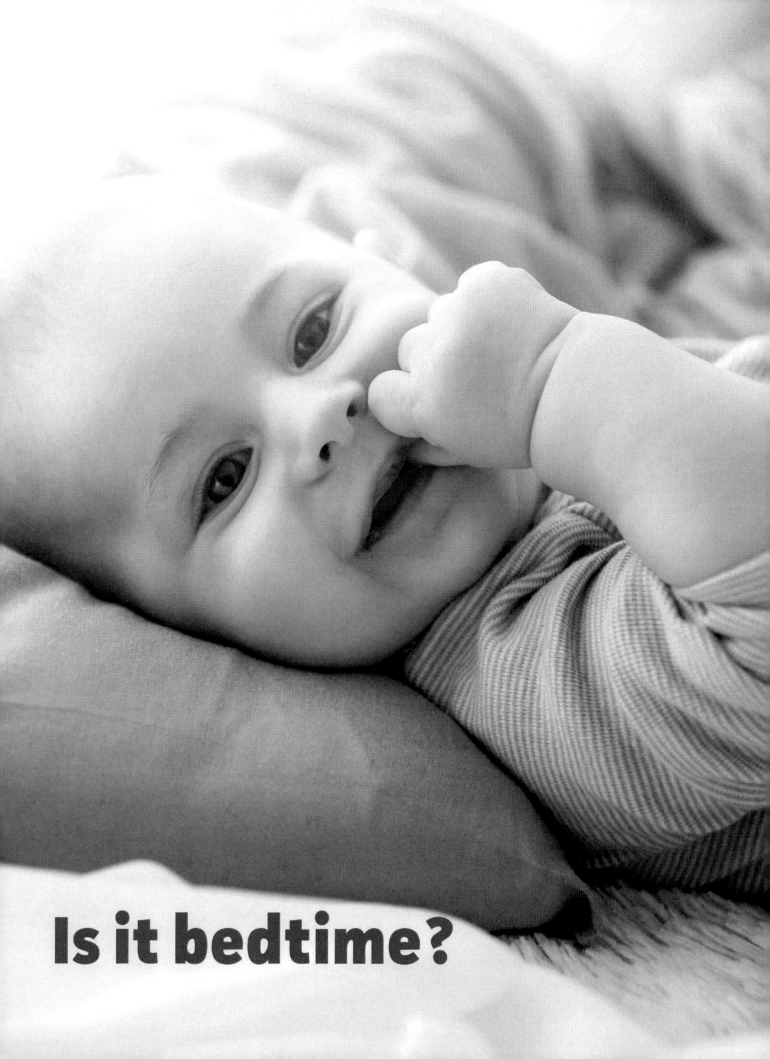

Is it bedtime?

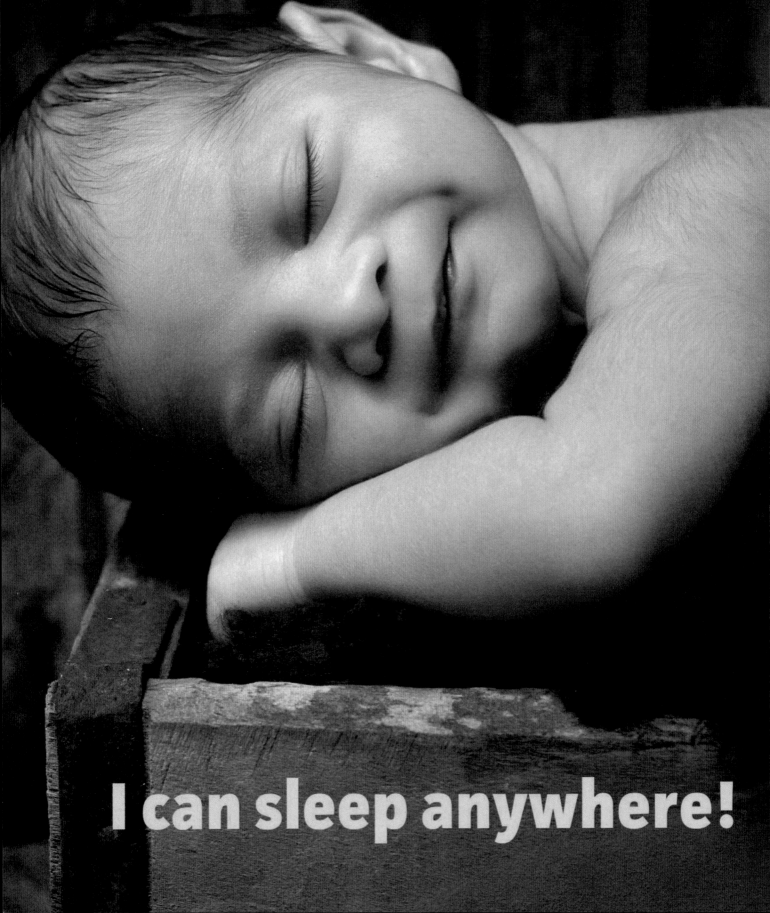

I can sleep anywhere!

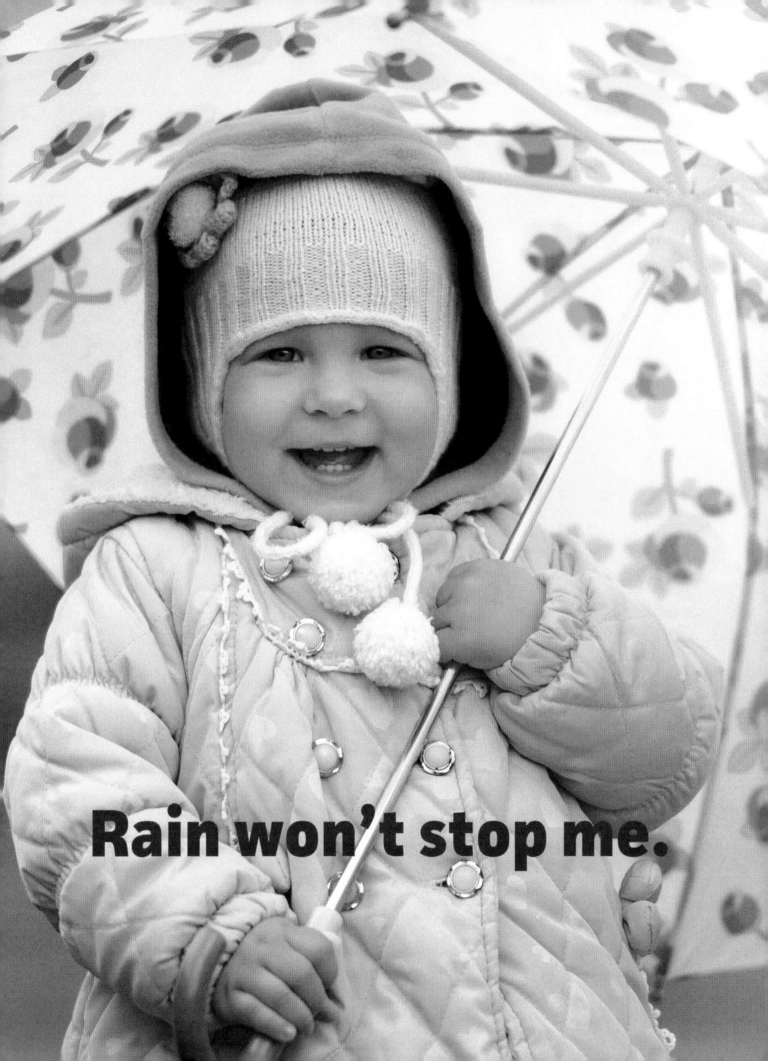

Rain won't stop me.

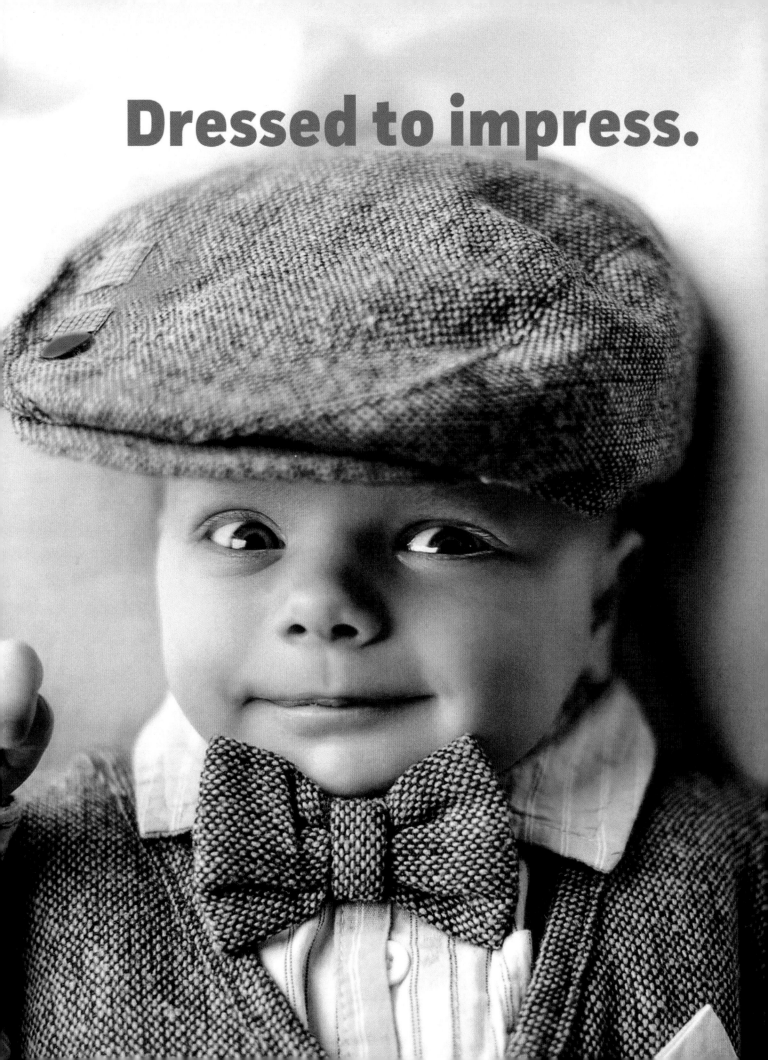

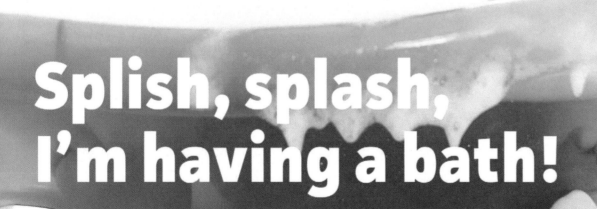

Splish, splash, I'm having a bath!

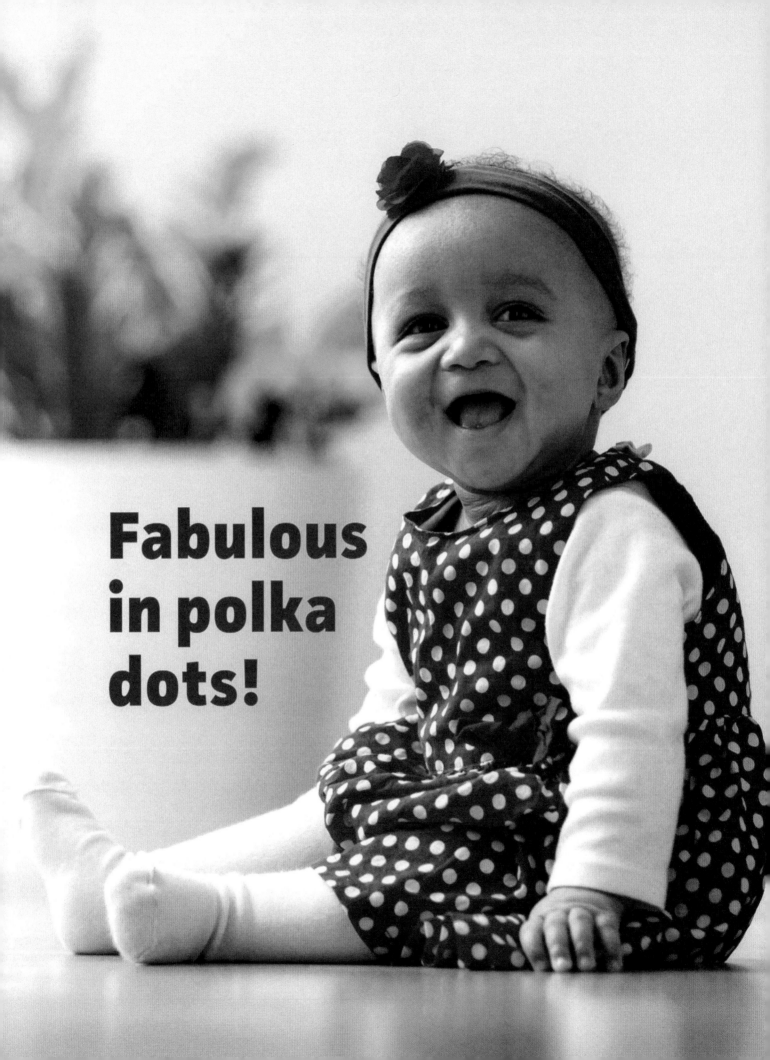

Fabulous in polka dots!

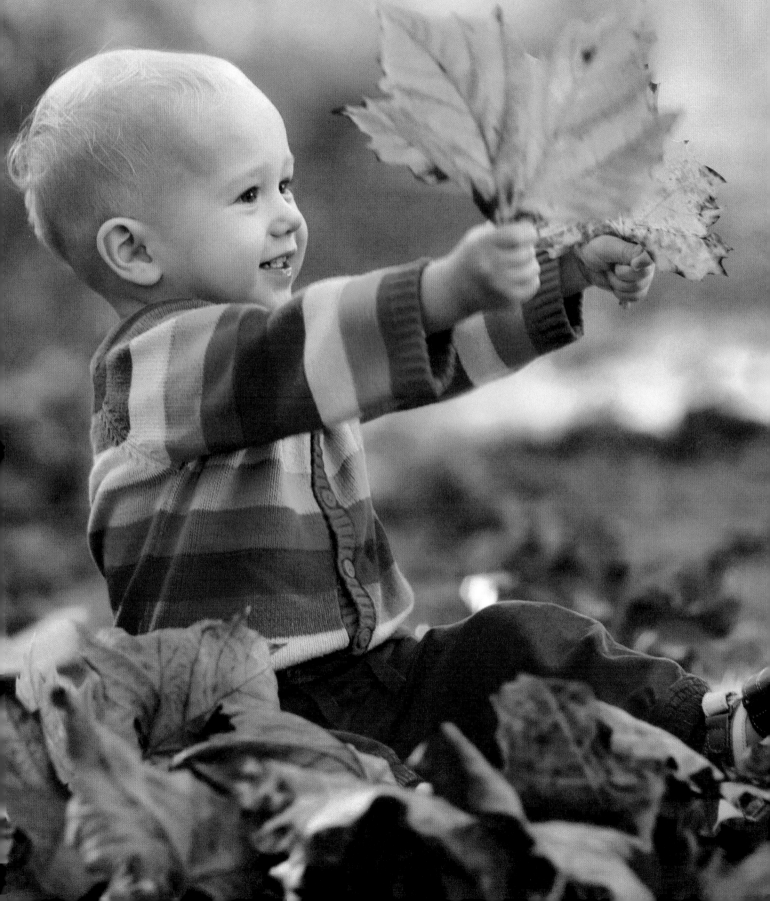

Hear the leaves crunch!

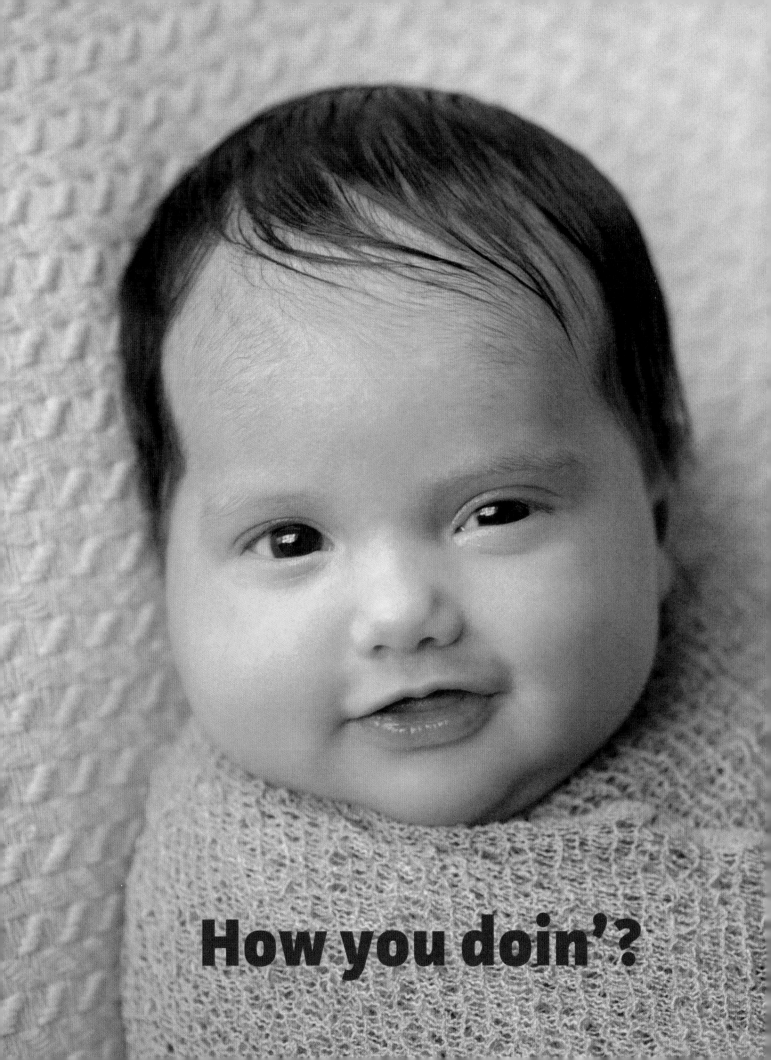

How you doin'?

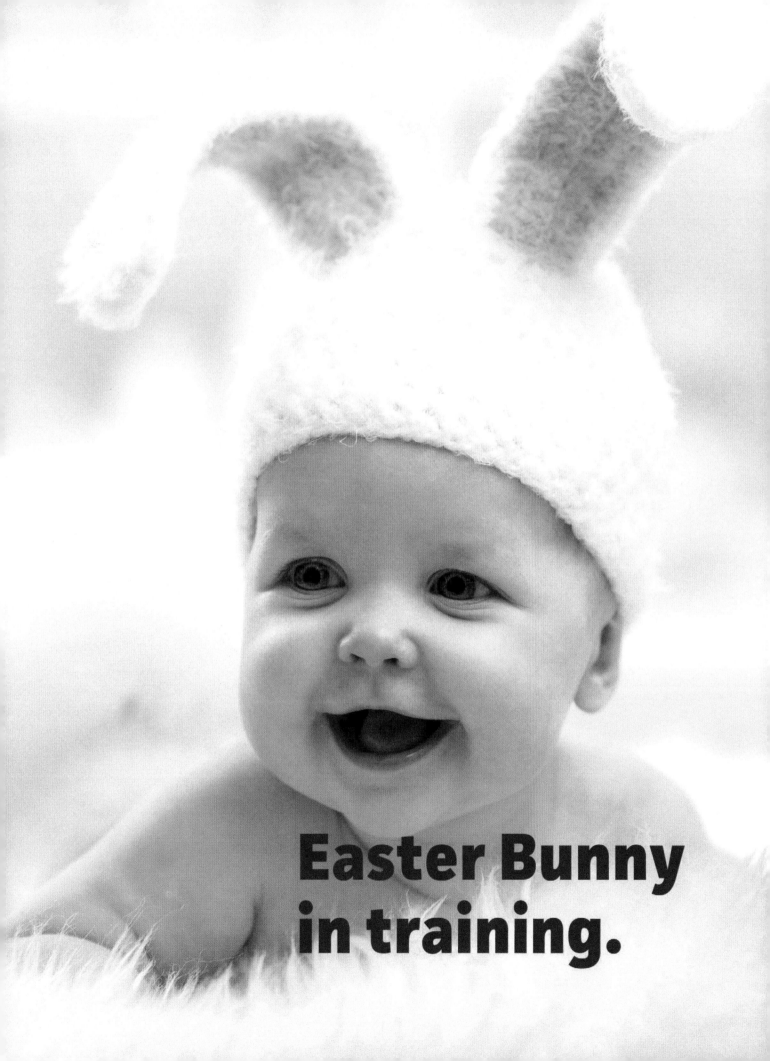

Easter Bunny in training.

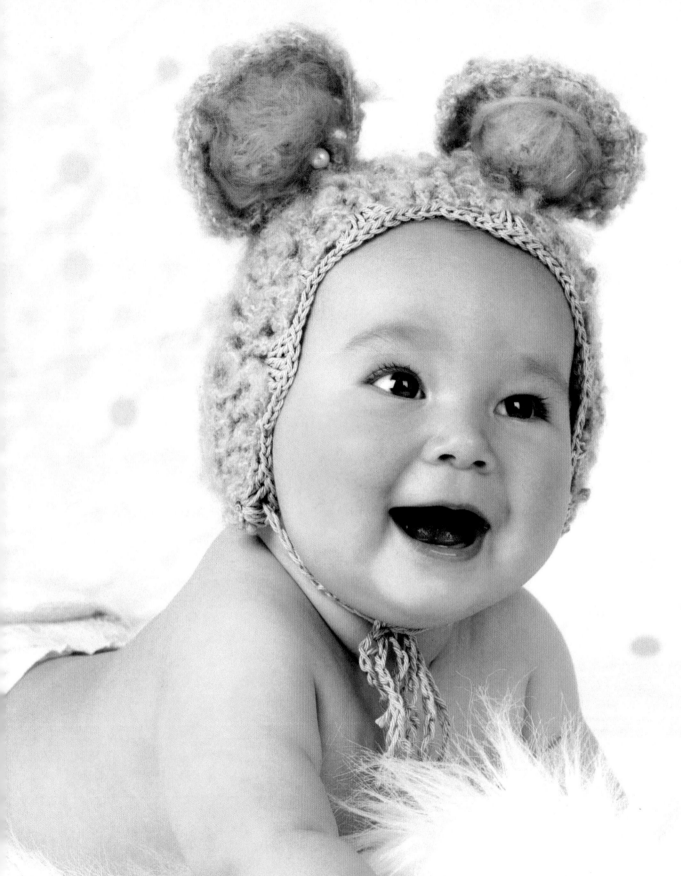

Cute as a button.

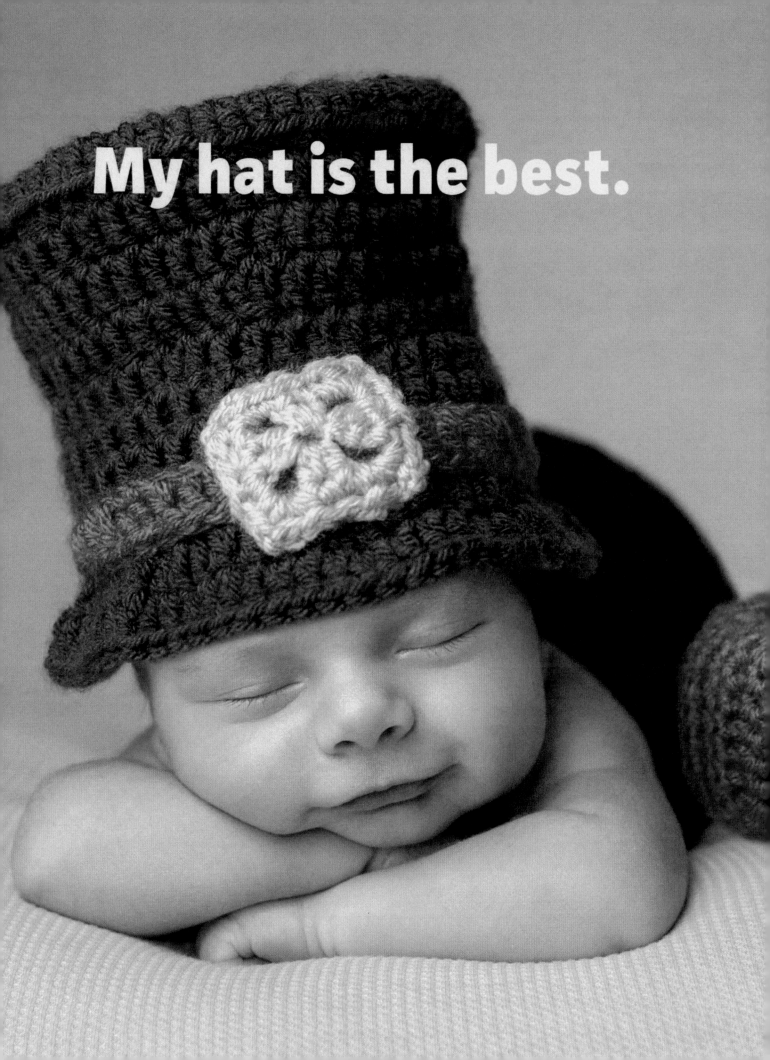

My hat is the best.

Did Santa come, yet?

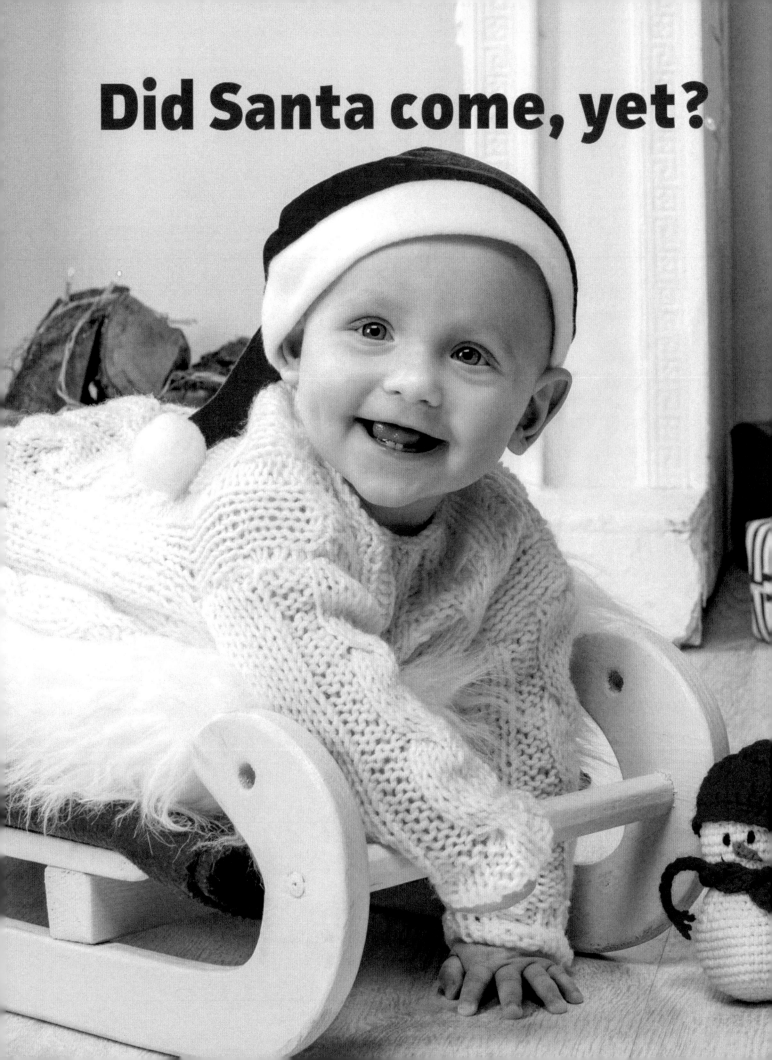

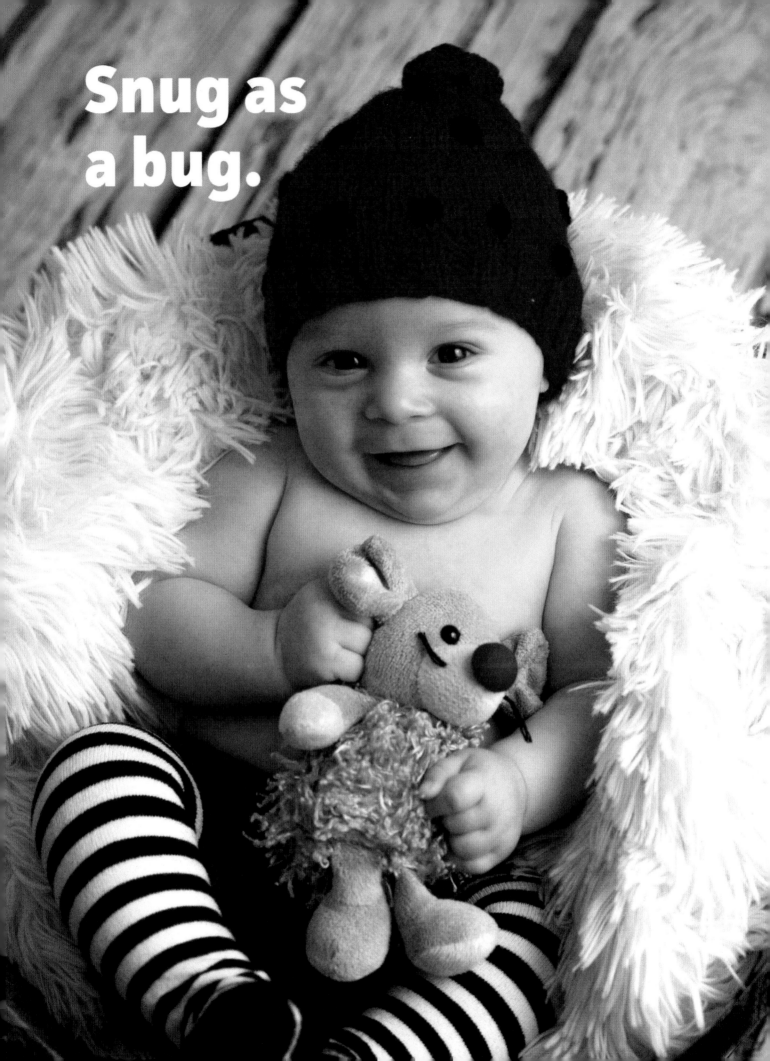

Snug as
a bug.

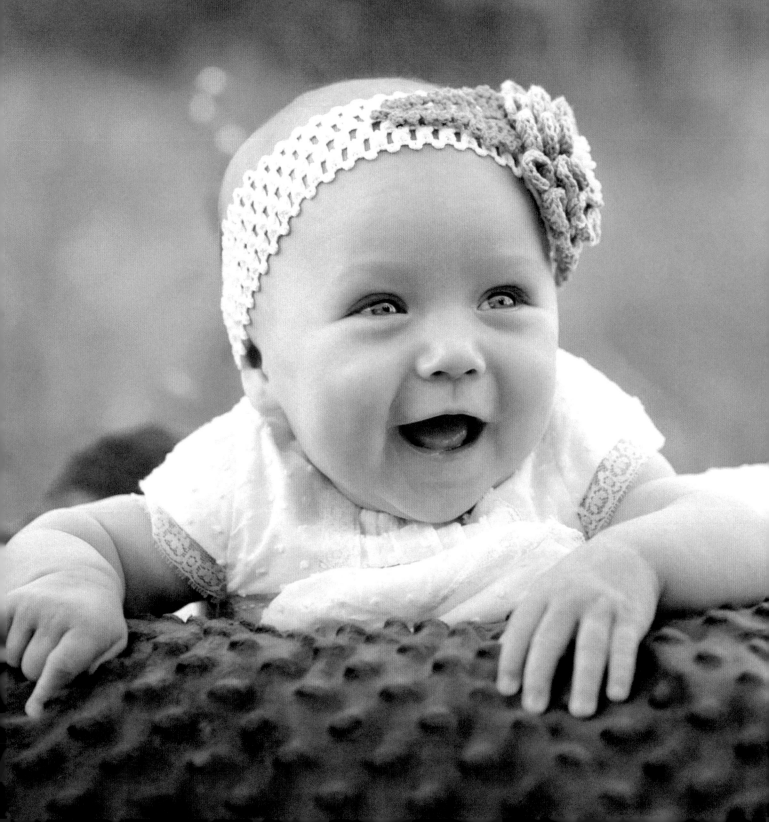

There's nothing better than spring.

An apple a day...

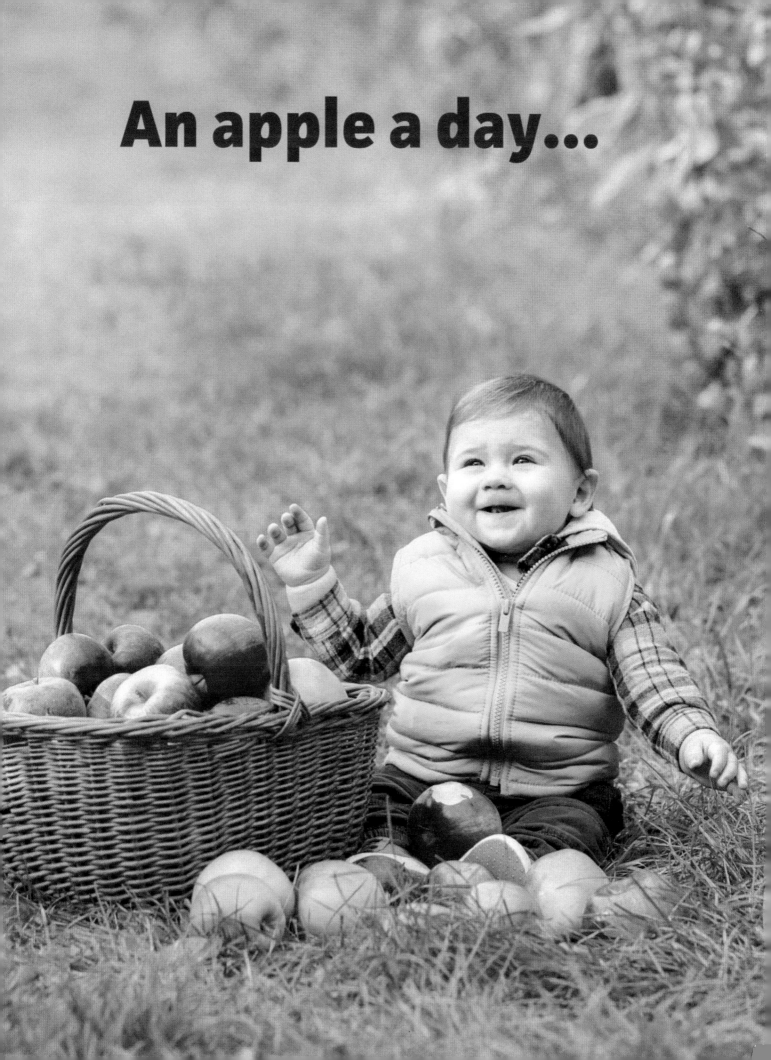

Let's go for a stroll.

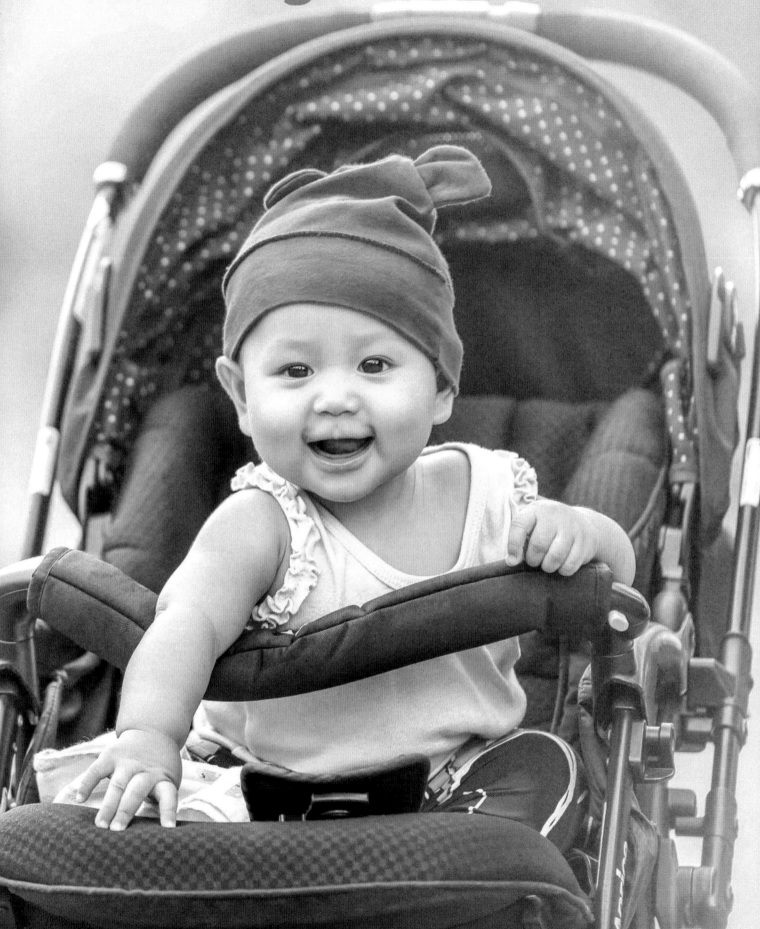

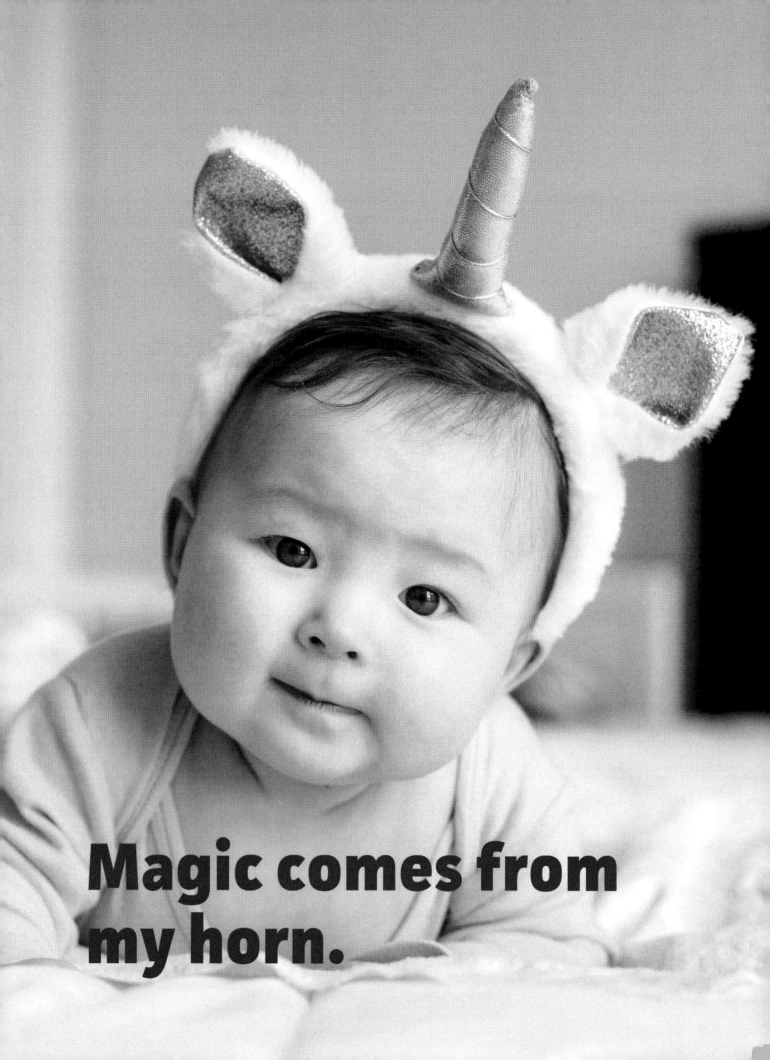

Magic comes from my horn.

Best hiding spot ever.

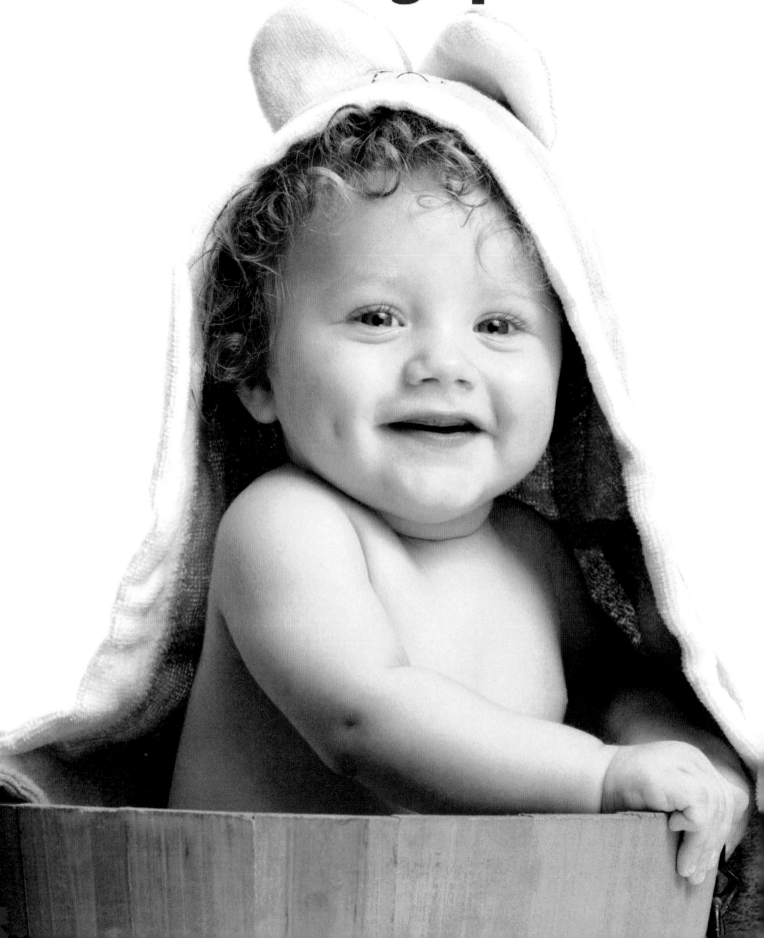

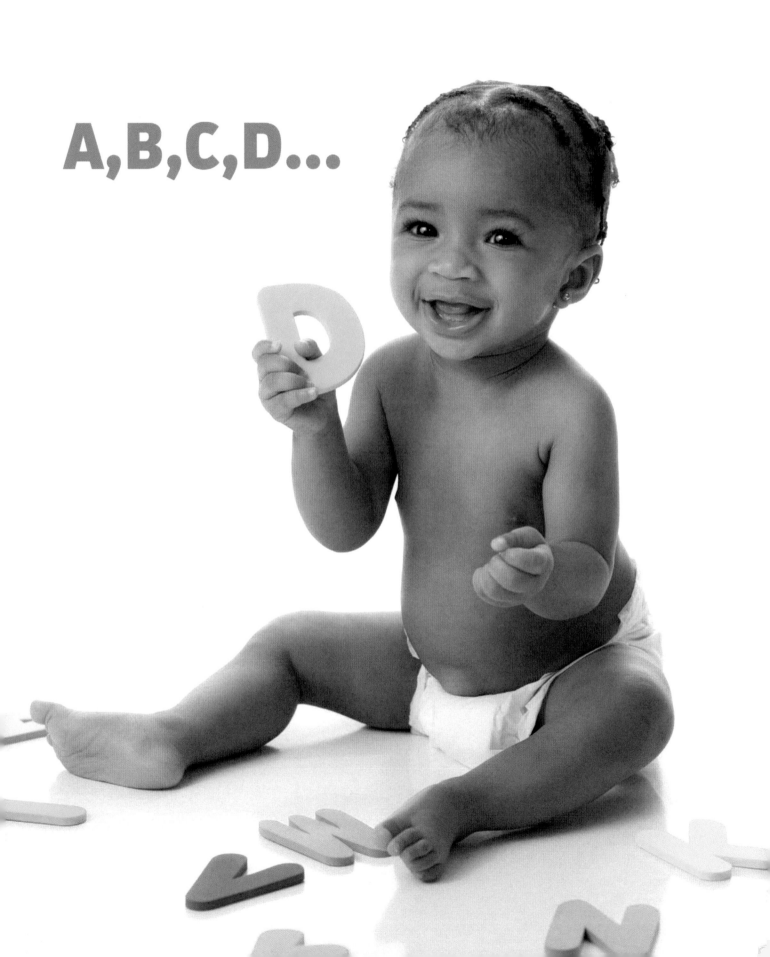

A,B,C,D...

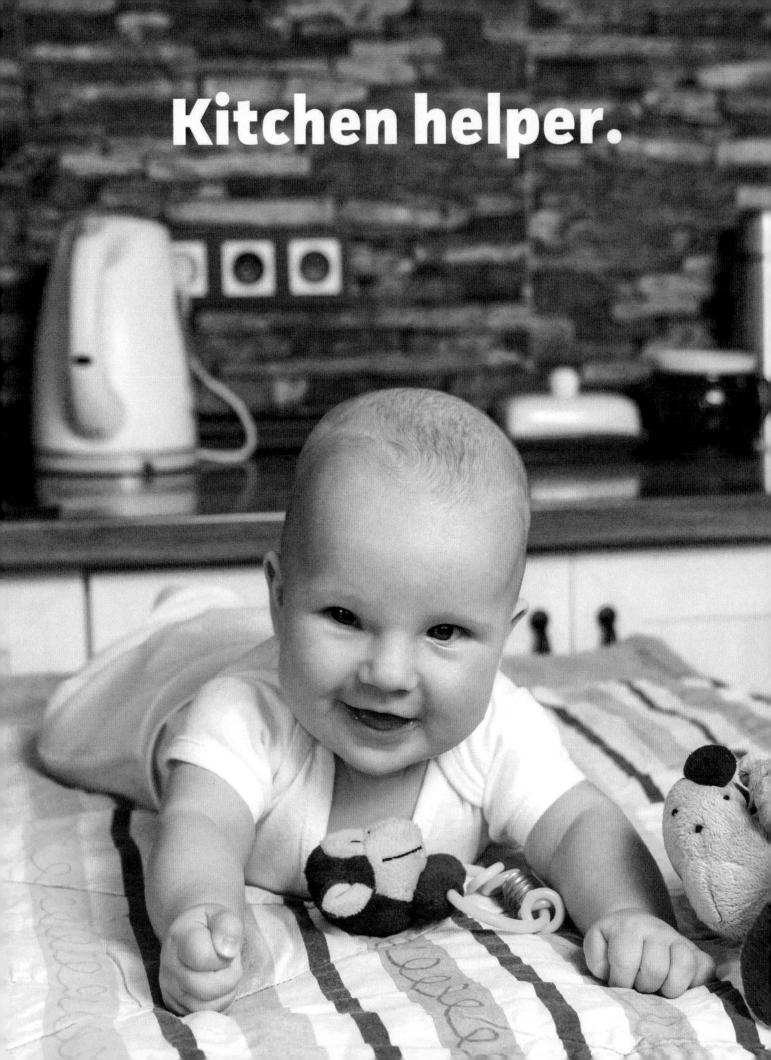

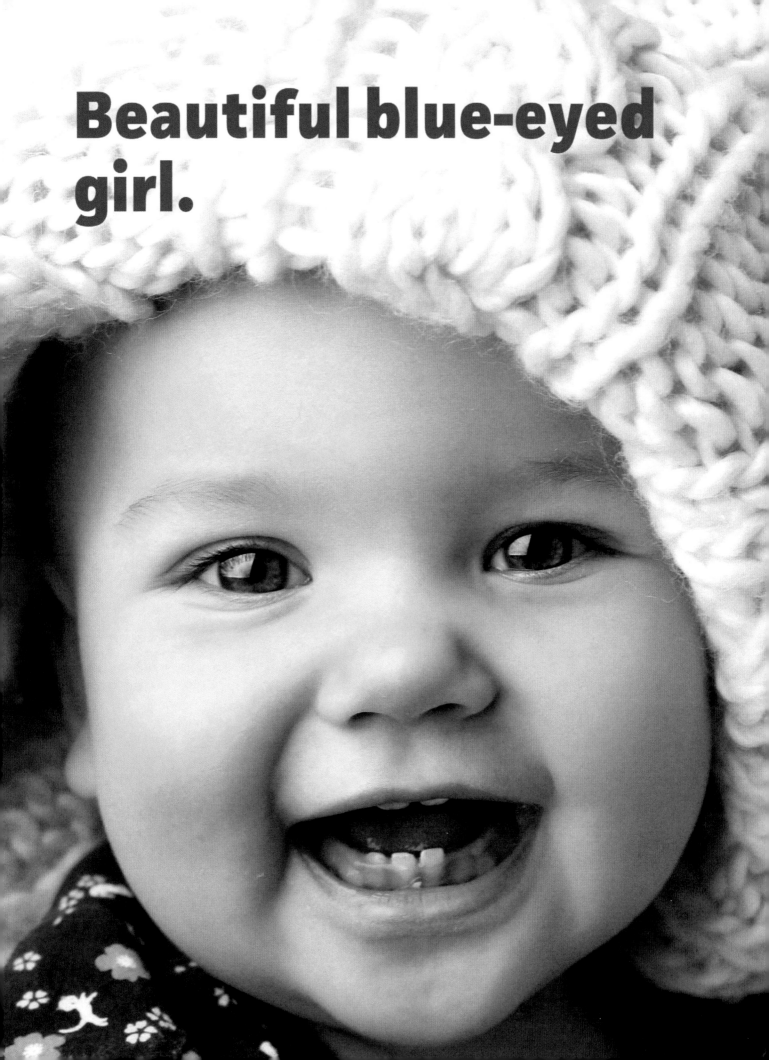

Beautiful blue-eyed girl.

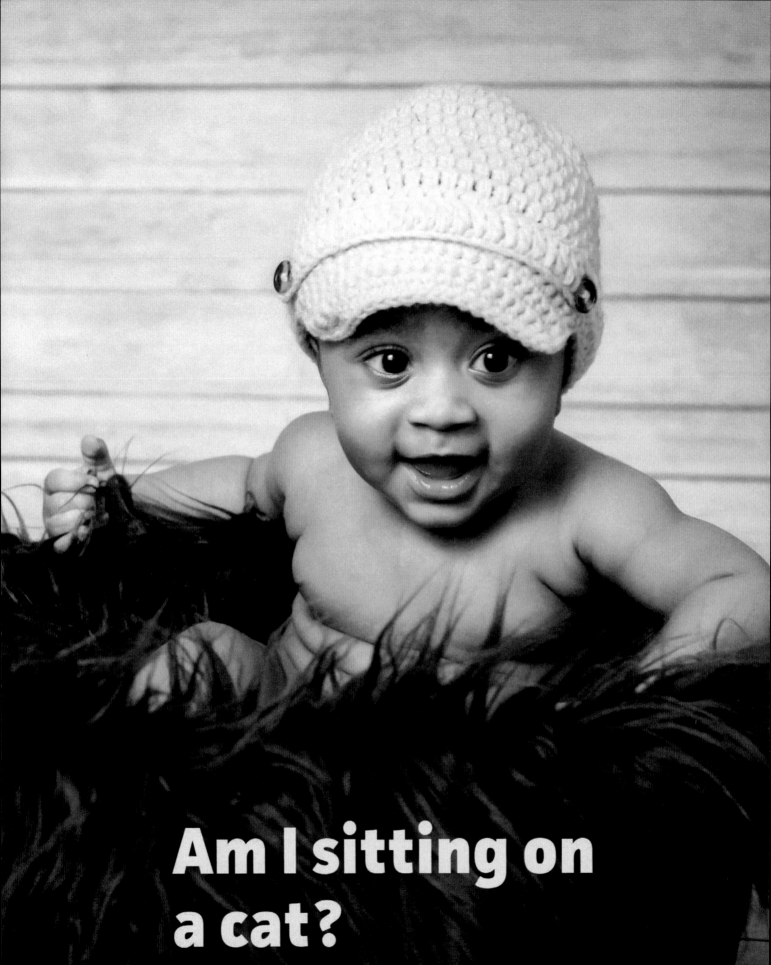

Am I sitting on a cat?

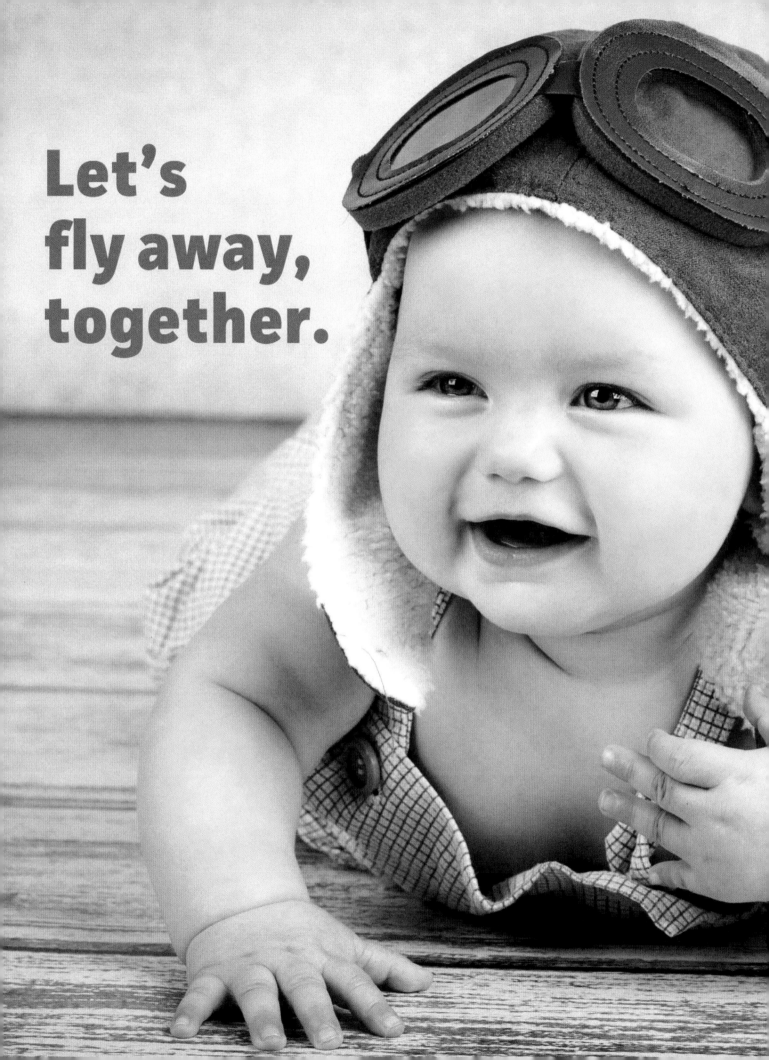

Let's
fly away,
together.

Made in the USA
San Bernardino, CA
16 February 2020